ABIDE IN CHRIST
&
THE TRUE VINE

DELUXE VERSION OF ANDREW MURRAY CLASSICS

By Andrew Murray
1897

Compiled by
RR

Sponsored By

Holy Land With RR
http://www.HolyLandWithRR.com

Learn Piano Hymns & Gospel Songs
http://www.LearnPianoWithRosa.com

From the Desk of Editor

From the Desk of Editor

I want to take this opportunity to thank you for buying my eBook.

If you had liked my eBook, please give me a feedback and drop me a review in Amazon.

I have many other similar books like this one.

Click here to visit my Collection of Books

Connect with us in these 2 Websites & Facebook:

Holy Land With RR Website

Learn to Play Piano & Gospel Hymns

Like Me in Facebook

Write to us and we look forward to hear from you,
RR Publishing Company

TABLE OF CONTENTS

Book One: ABIDE IN CHRIST

Book Two: The True Vine

Get Discounts From My Bookshelf

ABIDE IN CHRIST

John 15:1-12

1 I am the true vine, and my Father is the husbandman.
2 Every branch in me that beareth not fruit he taketh away;
and every branch that beareth fruit, he purgeth it, that it may
bring forth more fruit.
3 Now ye are clean through the word which I have spoken
unto you.
4 Abide in me, and I in you. As the branch cannot bear fruit of
itself, except it abide in the vine; no more can ye, except ye
abide in me.
5 I am the vine, ye are the branches: he that abideth in me,
and I in him, the same bringeth forth much fruit: for without me
ye can do nothing.
6 If a man abide not in me, he is cast forth as a branch, and is
withered; and men gather them, and cast them into the fire,
and they are burned.
7 If ye abide in me, and my words abide in you, ye shall ask
what ye will, and it shall be done unto you.
8 Herein is my Father glorified, that ye bear much fruit; so
shall ye be my disciples.
9 As the Father hath loved me, so have I loved you: continue
ye in my love.
10. If ye keep my commandments, ye shall abide in my love;
even as I have kept my Father's commandments and abide in
his love.

—

11 These things have I spoken unto you, that my joy might remain in you, and that your joy might be full.
12 This is my commandment, That ye love one another, as I have loved you.

Preface -- By Andrew Murray

During the life of Jesus on earth, the word He chiefly used when speaking of the relations of the disciples to Himself was: "Follow me." When about to leave for heaven, He gave them a new word, in which their more intimate and spiritual union with Himself in glory should be expressed. That chosen word was: "Abide in me."

It is to be feared that there are many earnest followers of Jesus from whom the meaning of this word, with the blessed experience it promises, is very much hidden. While trusting in their Saviour for pardon and for help, and seeking to some extent to obey Him, they have hardly realized to what closeness of union, to what intimacy of fellowship, to what wondrous oneness of life and interest, He invited them when He said, "Abide in me." This is not only an unspeakable loss to themselves, but the Church and the world suffer in what they lose.

If we ask the reason why those who have indeed accepted the Saviour, and been made partakers of the renewing of the Holy Ghost, thus come short of the full salvation prepared for them, I am sure the answer will in very many cases be, that ignorance is the cause of the unbelief that fails of the inheritance. If, in our orthodox Churches, the abiding in Christ, the living union with Him, the experience of His daily and hourly presence and keeping, were preached with the same distinctness and urgency as His atonement and pardon through His blood, I am confident that many would be found to accept with gladness the invitation to such a life, and that its influence would be manifest in their experience of the purity and the power, the love and the joy, the fruit-bearing, and all the blessedness which the Saviour connected with the abiding in Him.

—

It is with the desire to help those who have not yet fully understood what the Saviour meant with His command, or who have feared that it was a life beyond their reach, that these meditations are now published. It is only by frequent repetition that a child learns its lessons. It is only by continuously fixing the mind for a time on some one of the lessons of faith, that the believer is gradually helped to take and thoroughly assimilate them. I have the hope that to some, especially young believers, it will be a help to come and for a month day after day spell over the precious words, "Abide in me," with the lessons connected with them in the parable of the Vine. Step by step we shall get to see how truly this promise-precept is meant for us, how surely grace is provided to enable us to obey it, how indispensable the experience of its blessing is to a healthy Christian life, and how unspeakable the blessings are that flow from it. As we listen, and meditate, and pray -- as we surrender ourselves, and accept in faith the whole Jesus as He offers Himself to us in it -- the Holy Spirit will make the word to be spirit and life; this word of Jesus, too, will become to us the power of God unto salvation, and through it will come the faith that grasps the long desired blessing.

I pray earnestly that our gracious Lord may be pleased to bless this little book, to help those who seek to know Him fully, as He has already blessed it in its original issue in a different (the Dutch) language. I pray still more earnestly that He would, by whatever means, make the multitudes of His dear children who are still living divided lives, to see how He claims them wholly for Himself, and how the wholehearted surrender to abide in Him alone brings the joy unspeakable and full of glory. Oh, let each of us who has begun to taste the sweetness of this life, yield himself wholly to be a witness to the grace and power of our Lord to keep us united with Himself, and seek by word and walk to win others to follow Him fully. It is only in such fruitbearing that our own abiding can be maintained.

—

9

In conclusion, I ask to be permitted to give one word of advice to my reader. It is this. It needs time to grow into Jesus the Vine: do not expect to abide in Him unless you will give Him that time. It is not enough to read God's Word, or meditations as here offered, and when we think we have hold of the thoughts, and have asked God for His blessing, to go out in the hope that the blessing will abide. No, it needs day by day time with Jesus and with God. We all know the need of time for our meals each day -- every workman claims his hour for dinner; the hurried eating of so much food is not enough. If we are to live through Jesus, we must feed on Him (John 6:57); we must thoroughly take in and assimilate that heavenly food the Father has given us in His life. Therefore, my brother, who would learn to abide in Jesus, take time each day, ere you read, and while you read, and after you read, to put yourself into living contact with the living Jesus, to yield yourself distinctly and consciously to His blessed influence; so will you give Him the opportunity of taking hold of you, of drawing you up and keeping you safe in His almighty life.

And now, to all God's children whom He allows me the privilege of pointing to the Heavenly Vine, I offer my fraternal love and salutations, with the prayer that to each one of them may be given the rich and full experience of the blessedness of abiding in Christ. And may the grace of Jesus, and the love of God, and the fellowship of the Holy Spirit, be their daily portion. Amen.

Chapter 1 -- All You Who Have Come To Him

"Come unto me." -- Matt.11:28
"Abide in me." -- John 15:4

It Is to you who have heard and hearkened to the call, "Come unto me," that this new invitation comes, "Abide in me." The message comes from the same loving Saviour. You doubtless have never repented having come at His call. You experienced that His word was truth; all His promises He fulfilled; He made you partakers of the blessings and the joy of His love. Was not His welcome most hearty, His pardon full and free, His love most sweet and precious? You more than once, at your first coming to Him, had reason to say, "The half was not told me."

And yet you have had to complain of disappointment: as time went on, your expectations were not realized. The blessings you once enjoyed were lost; the love and joy of your first meeting with your Saviour, instead of deepening, have become faint and feeble. And often you have wondered what the reason could be, that with such a Saviour, so mighty and so loving, your experience of salvation should not have been a fuller one.

The answer is very simple. You wandered from Him. The blessings He bestows are all connected with His "Come to ME," and are only to be enjoyed in close fellowship with Himself. You either did not fully understand, or did not rightly remember, that the call meant, "Come to me to stay with me." And yet this was in very deed His object and purpose when first He called you to Himself. It was not to refresh you for a few short hours after your conversion with the joy of His love and deliverance, and then to send you forth to wander in sadness and sin. He had destined you to something better than a short-lived blessedness, to be enjoyed only in times of special earnestness and prayer, and then to pass away, as you had to return to those duties in which far the greater part of life has to be spent. No, indeed; He had prepared for you an abiding dwelling with Himself, where your whole life and every moment of it might be spent, where the work of your daily life might be done, and where all the while you might be enjoying unbroken communion with Himself. It was even this He meant when to that first word, "Come to me," He added this, "Abide in me." As earnest and faithful, as loving and tender, as the compassion that breathed in that blessed "Come," was the grace that added this no less blessed "Abide." As mighty as the attraction with which that first word drew you, were the bonds with which this second, had you but listened to it, would have kept you. And as great as were the blessings with which that coming was rewarded, so large, yea, and much greater, were the treasures to which that abiding would have given you access.

And observe especially, it was not that He said, "Come to me and abide with me," but, "Abide in me." The intercourse was not only to be unbroken, but most intimate and complete. He opened His arms, to press you to His bosom; He opened His heart, to welcome you there; He opened up all His divine fulness of life and love, and offered to take you up into its fellowship, to make you wholly one with Himself. There was a depth of meaning you cannot yet realize in His words: "Abide IN ME."

And with no less earnestness than He had cried, "Come to me," did He plead, had you but noticed it, "Abide in me." By every motive that had induced you to come, did He beseech you to abide. Was it the fear of sin and its curse that first drew you? the pardon you received on first coming could, with all the blessings flowing from it, only be confirmed and fully enjoyed on abiding in Him.

Was it the longing to know and enjoy the Infinite Love that was calling you? the first coming gave but single drops to taste -- 'tis only the abiding that can really satisfy the thirsty soul, and give to drink of the rivers of pleasure that are at His right hand. Was it the weary longing to be made free from the bondage of sin, to become pure and holy, and so to find rest, the rest of God for the soul? this too can only be realized as you abide in Him -- only abiding in Jesus gives rest in Him.

Or if it was the hope of an inheritance in glory, and an everlasting home in the presence of the Infinite One: the true preparation for this,as well as its blessed foretaste in this life, are granted only to those who abide in Him. In very truth, there is nothing that moved you to come, that does not plead with thousandfold greater force: "Abide in Him." You did well to come; you do better to abide. Who would, after seeking the King's palace, be content to stand in the door, when he is invited in to dwell in the King's presence, and share with Him in all the glory of His royal life? Oh, let us enter in and abide, and enjoy to the full all the rich supply His wondrous love hath prepared for us!

And yet I fear that there are many who have indeed come to Jesus, and who yet have mournfully to confess that they know but little of this blessed abiding in Him. With some the reason is, that they never fully understood that this was the meaning of the Saviour's call. With others, that though they heard the word, they did not know that such a life of abiding fellowship was possible, and indeed within their reach. Others will say that, though they did believe that such a life was possible, and seek after it, they have never yet succeeded discovering the secret of its attainment. And others, again, alas! will confess that it is their own unfaithfulness that has kept them from the enjoyment of the blessing. When the Saviour would have kept them, they were not found ready to stay; they were not prepared to give up everything, and always, only, wholly to abide in Jesus.

To all such I come now in the name of Jesus, their Redeemer and mine, with the blessed message: "Abide in me." In His name I invite them to come, and for a season meditate with me daily on its meaning, its lessons, its claims, and its promises. I know how many, and, to the young believer, how difficult, the questions are which suggest themselves in connection with it.

There is especially the question, with its various aspects, to the possibility, in the midst of wearying work and continual distraction, of keeping up, or rather being kept in, the abiding communion. I do not undertake to remove all difficulties; this Jesus Christ Himself alone must do by His Holy Spirit. But what I would fain by the grace of God be permitted to do is, to repeat day by day the Master's blessed command, "Abide in me," until it enter the heart and find a place there, no more to be forgotten or neglected. I would fain that in the light of Holy Scripture we should Meditate on its meaning, until the understanding, that gate to the heart, opens to apprehend something of what it offers and expects.

So we shall discover the means of its attainment, and learn to know what keeps us from it, and what can help us to it. So we shall feel its claims, and be compelled to acknowledge that there can be no true allegiance to our King without simply and heartily accepting this one, too, of His commands. So we shall gaze on its blessedness, until desire be inflamed, and the will with all its energies be roused to claim and possess the unspeakable blessing.

Come, my brethren, and let us day by day set ourselves at His feet, and meditate on this word of His, with an eye fixed on Him alone. Let us set ourselves in quiet trust before Him, waiting to hear His holy voice -- the still small voice that is mightier than the storm that rends the rocks -- breathing its quickening spirit within us, as He speaks: "Abide in me." The soul that truly hears Jesus Himself speak the word, receives with the word the power to accept and to hold the blessing He offers.

And it may please Thee, blessed Saviour, indeed, to speak to us; let each of us hear Thy blessed voice. May the feeling of our deep need, and the faith of Thy wondrous love, combined with the sight of the wonderfully blessed life Thou art waiting to bestow upon us, constrain us to listen and to obey, as often as Thou speakest: "Abide in me." Let day by day the answer from our heart be clearer and fuller: "Blessed Saviour, I do abide in Thee. "

Chapter 2 -- And You Shall Find Rest To Your Souls

"Come unto me, and I will give you rest. Take my yoke upon you, and learn of me; and ye shall find rest to your souls"
-- Matt.11:28-29

Rest for the soul: Such was the first promise with which the Saviour sought to win the heavy-laden sinner. Simple though it appears, the promise is indeed as large and comprehensive as can be found. Rest for the soul -- does it not imply deliverance from every fear, the supply of every want, the fulfilment of every desire? And now nothing less than this is the prize with which the Saviour woos back the wandering one -- who is mourning that the rest has not been so abiding or so full as it had hoped -- to come back and abide in Him. Nothing but this was the reason that the rest has either not been found, or, if found, has been disturbed or lost again: you did not abide with, you did not abide in Him.

Have you ever noticed how, in the original invitation of the Saviour to come to Him, the promise of rest was repeated twice, with such a variation in the conditions as might have suggested that abiding rest could only be found in abiding nearness. First the Saviour says, "Come unto me, and I will give you rest"; the very moment you come, and believe, I will give you rest -- the rest of pardon and acceptance -- the rest in my love. But we know that all that God bestows needs time to become fully our own; it must be held fast, and appropriated, and assimilated into our inmost being; without this not even Christ's giving can make it our very own, in full experience and enjoyment. And so the Saviour repeats His promise, in words which clearly speak not so much of the initial rest with which He welcomes the weary one who comes, but of the deeper and personally appropriated rest of the soul that abides with Him. He now not only says, "Come unto me," but "Take my yoke upon you and learn of me"; become my scholars, yield ourselves to my training, submit in all things to my will, let your whole life be one with mine -- in other words, Abide in me. And then He adds, not only, "I will give," but "ye shall find rest to your souls." The rest He gave at coming will become something you have really found and made your very own -- the deeper the abiding rest which comes from longer acquaintance and closer fellowship, from entire surrender and deeper sympathy. "Take my yoke, and learn of me," "Abide in me" -- this is the path to abiding rest.

Do not these words of the Saviour discover what you have perhaps often sought in vain to know, how it is that the rest you at times enjoy is so often lost. It must have been this: you had not understood how entire surrender to Jesus is the secret of perfect rest. Giving up one's whole life to Him, for Him alone to rule and order it; taking up His yoke, and submitting to be led and taught, to learn of Him; abiding in Him, to be and do only what He wills -- these are the conditions of discipleship without which there can be no thought of maintaining the rest that was bestowed on first coming to Christ. The rest is in Christ, and not something He gives apart from Himself, and so it is only in having Him that the rest can really be kept and enjoyed.

17

It is because so many a young believer fails to lay hold of this truth that the rest so speedily passes away. With some it is that they really did not know; they were never taught how Jesus claims the undivided allegiance of the whole heart and life; how there is not a spot in the whole of life over which He does not wish to reign; how in the very least things His disciples must only seek to please Him. They did not know how entire the consecration was that Jesus claimed. With others, who had some idea of what a very holy life a Christian ought to lead, the mistake was a different one: they could not believe such a life to be a possible attainment. Taking, and bearing, and never for a moment laying aside the yoke of Jesus, appeared to them to require such a strain of effort, and such an amount of goodness, as to be altogether beyond their reach.

The very idea of always, all the day, abiding in Jesus, was too high -- something they might attain to after a life of holiness and growth, but certainly not what a feeble beginner was to start with. They did not know how, when Jesus said, "My yoke is easy," He spoke the truth; how just the yoke gives the rest, because the moment the soul yields itself to obey, the Lord Himself gives the strength and joy to do it. They did not notice how, when He said, "Learn of me," He added, "I am meek and lowly in heart," to assure them that His gentleness would meet their every need, and bear them as a mother bears her feeble child. Oh, they did not know that when He said, "Abide in me," He only asked the surrender to Himself, His almighty love would hold them fast, and keep and bless them. And so, as some had erred from the want of full consecration, so these failed because they did not fully trust. These two, consecration and faith, are the essential elements of the Christian life -- the giving up all to Jesus, the receiving all from Jesus. They are implied in each other; they are united in the one word -- surrender. A full surrender is to obey as well as to trust, to trust as well as to obey.

With such misunderstanding at the outset, it is no wonder that the disciple life was not one of such joy or strength as had been hoped. In some things you were led into sin without knowing it, because you had not learned how wholly Jesus wanted to rule you, and how you could not keep right for a moment unless you had Him very near you. In other things you knew what sin was, but had not the power to conquer, because you did not know or believe how entirely Jesus would take charge of you to keep and to help you.

Either way, it was not long before the bright joy of your first love was lost, and your path, instead of being like the path of the just, shining more and more unto the perfect day, became like Israel's wandering in the desert -- ever on the way, never very far, and yet always coming short of the promised rest. Weary soul, since so many years driven to and fro like the panting hart, O come and learn this day the lesson that there is a spot where safety and victory, where peace and rest, are always sure, and that that spot is always open to thee -- the heart of Jesus.

But, alas! I hear someone say, it is just this abiding in Jesus, always bearing His yoke, to learn of Him, that is so difficult, and the very effort to attain to this often disturbs the rest even more than sin or the world. What a mistake to speak thus, and yet how often the words are heard! Does it weary the traveller to rest in the house or on the bed where he seeks repose from his fatigue? Or is it a labour to a little child to rest in its mother's arms? Is it not the house that keeps the traveller within its shelter? do not the arms of the mother sustain and keep the little one? And so it is with Jesus. The soul has but to yield itself to Him, to be still and rest in the confidence that His love has undertaken, and that His faithfulness will perform, the work of keeping it safe in the shelter of His bosom. Oh, it is because the blessing is so great that our little hearts cannot rise to apprehend it; it is as if we cannot believe that Christ, the Almighty One, will in very deed teach and keep us all the day. And yet this is just what He has promised, for without this He cannot really give us rest. It is as our heart takes in this truth that, when He says, "Abide in me," "Learn of me," He really means it, and that it is His own work to keep us abiding when we yield ourselves to Him, that we shall venture to cast ourselves into the arms of His love, and abandon ourselves to His blessed keeping. It is not the yoke, but resistance to the yoke, that makes the difficulty; the whole-hearted surrender to Jesus, as at once our Master and our Keeper, finds and secures the rest.

Come, my brother, and let us this very day commence to accept the word of Jesus in all simplicity. It is a distinct command this: "Take my yoke, and learn of me, " "Abide in me. " A command has to be obeyed. The obedient scholar asks no questions about possibilities or results; he accepts every order in the confidence that his teacher has provided for all that is needed. The power and the perseverance to abide in the rest, and the blessing in abiding -- it belongs to the Saviour to see to this; 'tis mine to obey, 'tis His to provide.

Let us this day in immediate obedience accept the command, and answer boldly, "Saviour, I abide in Thee. At Thy bidding I take Thy yoke; I undertake the duty without delay; I abide in Thee." Let each consciousness of failure only give new urgency to the command, and teach us to listen more earnestly than ever till the Spirit again give us to hear the voice of Jesus saying, with a love and authority that inspire both hope and obedience, "Child, abide in me." That word, listened to as coming from Himself, will be an end of all doubting -- a divine promise of what shall surely be granted. And with ever-increasing simplicity its meaning will be interpreted. Abiding in Jesus is nothing but the giving up of oneself to be ruled and taught and led, and so resting in the arms of Everlasting Love.

Blessed rest! the fruit and the foretaste and the fellowship of God's own rest! found of them who thus come to Jesus to abide in Him. It is the peace of God, the great calm of the eternal world, that passeth all understanding, and that keeps the heart and mind. With this grace secured, we have strength for every duty, courage for every struggle, a blessing in every cross, and the joy of life eternal in death itself.

O my Saviour! if ever my heart should doubt or fear again, as if the blessing were too great to expect, or too high to attain, let me hear Thy voice to quicken my faith and obedience: "Abide in me"; "Take my yoke upon you, and learn of me; ye shall find rest to your souls."

Chapter 3 -- Trusting Him To Keep You

"I follow after, if that I may apprehend that for which I also am apprehended of Christ Jesus." – Phil.3:12

More than one admits that it is a sacred duty and a blessed privilege to abide in Christ, but shrinks back continually before the question: Is it possible, a life of unbroken fellowship with the Saviour? Eminent Christians, to whom special opportunities of cultivating this grace have been granted, may attain to it; for the large majority of disciples, whose life, by a divine appointment, is so fully occupied with the affairs of this life, it can scarce be expected. The more they hear of this life, the deeper their sense of its glory and blessedness, and there is nothing they would not sacrifice to be made partakers of it. But they are too weak, too unfaithful -- they never can attain to it.

Dear souls! how little they know that the abiding in Christ is just meant for the weak, and so beautifully suited to their feebleness. It is not the doing of some great thing, and does not demand that we first lead a very holy and devoted life. No, it is simply weakness entrusting itself to a Mighty One to be kept -- the unfaithful one casting self on One who is altogether trustworthy and true. Abiding in Him is not a work that we have to do as the condition for enjoying His salvation, but a consenting to let Him do all for us, and in us, and through us. It is a work He does for us -- the fruit and the power of His redeeming love. Our part is simply to yield, to trust, and to wait for what He has engaged to perform.

It is this quiet expectation and confidence, resting on the word of Christ that in Him there is an abiding place prepared, which is so sadly wanting among Christians. They scarce take the time or the trouble to realize that when He says "Abide IN ME," He offers Himself, the Keeper of Israel that slumbers not nor sleeps, with all His power and love, as the living home of the soul, where the mighty influences of His grace will be stronger to keep than all their feebleness to lead astray. The idea they have of grace is this -- that their conversion and pardon are God's work, but that now, in gratitude to God, it is their work to live as Christians, and follow Jesus. There is always the thought of a work that has to be done, and even though they pray for help, still the work is theirs. They fail continually, and become hopeless; and the despondency only increases the helplessness. No, wandering one; as it was Jesus who drew you when He spake "Come," so it is Jesus who keeps you when He says "Abide." The grace to come and the grace to abide are alike from Him alone. That word Come, heard, meditated on, accepted, was the cord of love that drew you nigh; that word Abide is even so the band with which He holds you fast and binds you to Himself. Let the soul but take time to listen to the voice of Jesus. "In me," He says, "is thy place -- in my almighty arms. It is I who love thee so, who speak Abide in me; surely thou canst trust me." The voice of Jesus entering and dwelling in the soul cannot but call for the response: "Yes, Saviour, in Thee I can, I will abide."

23

Abide in me: These words are no law of Moses, demanding from the sinful what they cannot perform. They are the command of love, which is ever only a promise in a different shape. Think of this until all feeling of burden and fear and despair pass away, and the first thought that comes as you hear of abiding in Jesus be one of bright and joyous hope: it is for me, I know I shall enjoy it. You are not under the law, with its inexorable Do, but under grace, with its blessed Believe what Christ will do for you. And if the question be asked, "But surely there is something for us to do?" the answer is, "Our doing and working are but the fruit of Christ's work in us." It is when the soul becomes utterly passive, looking and resting on what Christ is to do, that its energies are stirred to their highest activity, and that we work most effectually because we know that He works in us. It is as we see in that word IN ME the mighty energies of love reaching out after us to have us and to hold us, that all the strength of our will is roused to abide in Him.

This connection between Christ's work and our work is beautifully expressed in the words of Paul: "I follow after, if that I may apprehend that whereunto I also am apprehended of Christ Jesus." It was because he knew that the mighty and the faithful One had grasped him with the glorious purpose of making him one with Himself, that he did his utmost to grasp the glorious prize. The faith, the experience, the full assurance, "Christ hath apprehended me," gave him the courage and the strength to press on and apprehend that whereunto he was apprehended. Each new insight of the great end for which Christ had apprehended and was holding him, roused him afresh to aim at nothing less.

Paul's expression, and its application to the Christian life, can be best understood if we think of a father helping his child to mount the side of some steep precipice. The father stands above, and has taken the son by the hand to help him on. He points him to the spot on which he will help him to plant his feet, as he leaps upward. The leap would be too high and dangerous for the child alone; but the father's hand is his trust, and he leaps to get hold of the point for which his father has taken hold of him. It is the father's strength that secures him and lifts him up, and so urges him to use his utmost strength.

Such is the relation between Christ and you, O weak and trembling believer! Fix first your eyes on the whereunto for which He has apprehended you. It is nothing less than a life of abiding, unbroken fellowship with Himself to which He is seeking to lift you up. All that you have already received -- pardon and peace, the Spirit and His grace -- are but preliminary to this. And all that you see promised to you in the future -- holiness and fruitfulness and glory everlasting -- are but its natural outcome. Union with Himself, and so with the Father, is His highest object. Fix your eye on this, and gaze until it stand out before you clear and unmistakeable: Christ's aim is to have me abiding in Him.

And then let the second thought enter your heart: Unto this I am apprehended of Christ. His almighty power hath laid hold on me, and offers now to lift me up to where He would have me. Fix your eyes on Christ. Gaze on the love that beams in those eyes, and that asks whether you cannot trust Him, who sought and found and brought you nigh, now to keep you. Gaze on that arm of power, and say whether you have reason to be assured that He is indeed able to keep you abiding in Him.

And as you think of the spot whither He points -- the blessed whereunto for which He apprehended you -- and keep your gaze fixed on Himself, holding you and waiting to lift you up, O say, could you not this very day take the upward step, and rise to enter upon this blessed life of abiding in Christ? Yes, begin at once, and say, "O my Jesus, if Thou biddest me, and if Thou engagest to lift and keep me there, I will venture. Trembling, but trusting, I will say: Jesus, I do abide in Thee."

My beloved fellow-believer, go, and take time alone with Jesus, and say this to Him. I dare not speak to you about abiding in Him for the mere sake of calling forth a pleasing religious sentiment. God's truth must at once be acted on. O yield yourself this very day to the blessed Saviour in the surrender of the one thing He asks of you: give up yourself to abide in Him. He Himself will work it in you. You can trust Him to keep you trusting and abiding.

And if ever doubts again arise, or the bitter experience of failure tempt you to despair, just remember where Paul found His strength: "I am apprehended of Jesus Christ." In that assurance you have a fountain of strength. From that you can look up to the whereunto on which He has set His heart, and set yours there too. From that you gather confidence that the good work He hath begun He will also perform. And in that confidence you will gather courage, day by day, afresh to say, " `I follow on, that I may also apprehend that for which I am apprehended of Christ Jesus.' It is because Jesus has taken hold of me, and because Jesus keeps me, that I dare to say: Saviour, I abide in Thee."

Chapter 4 - As The Branch In The Vine

"I am the vine, ye are the branches."-John 15:5

It was in connection with the parable of the Vine that our Lord first used the expression, "Abide in me." That parable, so simple, and yet so rich in its teaching, gives us the best and most complete illustration of the meaning of our Lord's command, and the union to which He invites us.

The parable teaches us the nature of that union. The connection between the vine and the branch is a living one. No external, temporary union will suffice; no work of man can effect it: the branch, whether an original or an engrafted one, is such only by the Creator's own work, in virtue of which the life, the sap, the fatness, and the fruitfulness of the vine communicate themselves to the branch. And just so it is with the believer too. His union with his Lord is no work of human wisdom or human will, but an act of God, by which the closest and most complete life-union is effected between the Son of God and the sinner. "God hath sent forth the Spirit of His Son into your hearts." The same Spirit which dwelt and still dwells in the Son, becomes the life of the believer; in the unity of that one Spirit, and the fellowship of the same life which is in Christ, he is one with Him. As between the vine and branch, it is a life-union that makes them one.

The parable teaches us the completeness of the union. So close is the union between the vine and the branch, that each is nothing without the other, that each is wholly and only for the other.

Without the vine the branch can do nothing. To the vine it owes its right of place in the vineyard, its life and its fruitfulness. And so the Lord says, "Without me ye can do nothing." The believer can each day be pleasing to God only in that which he does through the power of Christ dwelling in him. The daily inflowing of the life-sap of the Holy Spirit is his only power to bring forth fruit. He lives alone in Him and is for each moment dependent on Him alone.

Without the branch the vine can also do nothing. A vine without branches can bear no fruit. No less indispensable than the vine to the branch, is the branch to the vine. Such is the wonderful condescension of the grace of Jesus, that just as His people are dependent on Him, He has made Himself dependent on them. Without His disciples He cannot dispense His blessing to the world; He cannot offer sinners the grapes of the heavenly Canaan. Marvel not! It is His own appointment; and this is the high honour to which He has called His redeemed ones, that as indispensable as He is to them in heaven, that from Him their fruit may be found, so indispensable are they to Him on earth, that through them His fruit may be found. Believers, meditate on this, until your soul bows to worship in presence of the mystery of the perfect union between Christ and the believer.

There is more: as neither vine nor branch is anything without the other, so is neither anything except for the other.

All the vine possesses belongs to the branches. The vine does not gather from the soil its fatness and its sweetness for itself -- all it has is at the disposal of the branches. As it is the parent, so it is the servant of the branches. And Jesus, to whom we owe our life, how completely does He give Himself for us and to us: "The glory Thou gavest me, I have given them"; "He that believeth in me, the works that I do shall he do also; and greater works shall he do." All His fullness and all His riches are for thee, O believer; for the vine does not live for itself, keeps nothing for itself, but exists only for the branches. All that Jesus is in heaven, He is for us: He has no interest there separate from ours; as our representative He stands before the Father.

And all the branch possesses belongs to the vine. The branch does not exist for itself, but to bear fruit that can proclaim the excellence of the vine: it has no reason of existence except to be of service to the vine. Glorious image of the calling of the believer, and the entireness of his consecration to the service of his Lord. As Jesus gives Himself so wholly over to him, he feels himself urged to be wholly his Lord's. Every power of his being, every moment of his life, every thought and feeling, belong to Jesus, that from Him and for Him he may bring forth fruit. As he realizes what the vine is to the branch, and what the branch is meant to be to the vine, he feels that he has but one thing to think of and to live for, and that is, the will, the glory, the work, the kingdom of his blessed Lord -- the bringing forth of fruit to the glory of His name.

The parable teaches us the object of the union. The branches are for fruit and fruit alone. "Every branch that beareth not fruit He taketh away." The branch needs leaves for the maintenance of its own life, and the perfection of its fruit: the fruit itself it bears to give away to those around. As the believer enters into his calling as a branch, he sees that he has to forget himself, and to live entirely for his fellowmen. To love them, to seek for them, and to save them, Jesus came: for this every branch on the Vine has to live as much as the Vine itself. It is for fruit, much fruit, that the Father has made us one with Jesus.

—

29

Wondrous parable of the Vine-unveiling the mysteries of the Divine love, of the heavenly life, of the world of Spirit -- how little have I understood thee! Jesus the living Vine in heaven, and I the living branch on earth! How little have I understood how great my need, but also how perfect my claim, to all His fullness! How little understood, how great His need, but also how perfect His claim, to my emptiness! Let me, in its beautiful light, study the wondrous union between Jesus and His people, until it becomes to me the guide into full communion with my beloved Lord. Let me listen and believe, until my whole being cries out, "Jesus is indeed to me the True Vine, bearing me, nourishing me, supplying me, using me, and filling me to the full to make me bring forth fruit abundantly." Then shall I not fear to say, "I am indeed a branch to Jesus, the True Vine, abiding in Him, resting on Him, waiting for Him, serving Him, and living only that through me, too, He may show forth the riches of His grace, and give His fruit to a perishing world."

It is when we try thus to understand the meaning of the parable, that the blessed command spoken in connection with it will come home to us in its true power. The thought of what the vine is to the branch, and Jesus to the believer, will give new force to the words, "Abide in me!" It will be as if He says, "Think, soul, how completely I belong to thee. I have joined myself inseparably to thee; all the fulness and fatness of the Vine are thine in very deed. Now thou once art in me, be assured that all I have is wholly thine. It is my interest and my honour to have thee a fruitful branch; only Abide in me. Thou art weak, but I am strong; thou art poor, but I am rich. Only abide in me; yield thyself wholly to my teaching and rule; simply trust my love, my grace, my promises. Only believe; I am wholly thine; I am the Vine, thou art the branch. Abide in me."

What sayest thou, O my soul? Shall I longer hesitate, or withhold consent? Or shall I not, instead of only thinking how hard and how difficult it is to live like a branch of the True Vine, because I thought of it as something I had to accomplish -- shall I not now begin to look upon it as the most blessed and joyful thing under heaven? Shall I not believe that, now I once am in Him, He Himself will keep me and enable me to abide? On my part, abiding is nothing but the acceptance of my position, the consent to be kept there, the surrender of faith to the strong Vine still to hold the feeble branch. Yes, I will, I do abide in Thee, blessed Lord Jesus.

O Saviour, how unspeakable is Thy love! "Such knowledge is too wonderful for me: it is high, I cannot attain unto it." I can only yield myself to Thy love with the prayer that, day by day, Thou wouldest unfold to me somewhat of its precious mysteries, and so encourage and strengthen Thy loving disciple to do what his heart longs to do indeed -- ever, only, wholly to abide in Thee.

Chapter 5 -- As You Came To Him, By Faith

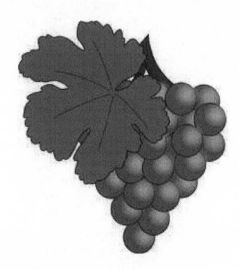

"As ye have received Christ Jesus the Lord, so walk ye in Him: rooted and built up in Him, and stablished in the faith, abounding therein. "Col.2:6-7

In these words the apostle teaches us the weighty lesson, that it is not only by faith that we first come to Christ and are united to Him, but that it is by faith that we are to be rooted and established in our union with Christ. Not less essential than for the commencement, is faith for the progress of the spiritual life. Abiding in Jesus can only be by faith.

There are earnest Christians who do not understand this; or, if they admit it in theory, they fail to realize its application in practice. They are very zealous for a free gospel, with our first acceptance of Christ, and justification by faith alone. But after this they think everything depends on our diligence and faithfulness. While they firmly grasp the truth, "The sinner shall be justified by faith," they have hardly found a place in their scheme for the larger truth, "The just shall live by faith." They have never understood what a perfect Saviour Jesus is, and how He will each day do for the sinner just as much as He did the first day when he came to Him. They know not that the life of grace is always and only a life of faith, and that in the relationship to Jesus the one daily and unceasing duty of the disciple is to believe, because believing is the one channel through which divine grace and strength flow out into the heart of man. The old nature of the believer remains evil and sinful to the last; it is only as he daily comes, all empty and helpless, to his Saviour to receive of His life and strength, that he can bring forth the fruits of righteousness to the glory of God. Therefore it is: "As ye have received Christ Jesus the Lord, so walk ye in Him: rooted in Him, and stablished in the faith, abounding therein." As you came to Jesus, so abide in Him, by faith.

And if you would know how faith is to be exercised in thus abiding in Jesus, to be rooted more deeply and firmly in Him, you have only to look back to the time when first you received Him. You remember well what obstacles at that time there appeared to be in the way of your believing. There was first your vileness and guilt: it appeared impossible that the promise of pardon and love could be for such a sinner. Then there was the sense of weakness and death: you felt not the power for the surrender and the trust to which you were called. And then there was the future: you dared not undertake to be a disciple of Jesus while you felt so sure that you could not remain standing, but would speedily again be unfaithful and fall. These difficulties were like mountains in your way. And how were they removed? Simply by the word of God. That word, as it were, compelled you to believe that, notwithstanding guilt in the past, and weakness in the present, and unfaithfulness in the future, the promise was sure that Jesus would accept and save you. On that word you ventured to come, and were not deceived: you found that Jesus did indeed accept and save.

Apply this, your experience in coming to Jesus, to the abiding in Him. Now, as then, the temptations to keep you from believing are many. When you think of your sins since you became a disciple, your heart is cast down with shame, and it looks as if it were too much to expect that Jesus should indeed receive you into perfect intimacy and the full enjoyment of His holy love. When you think how utterly, in times past, you have failed in keeping the most sacred vows, the consciousness of present weakness makes you tremble at the very idea of answering the Saviour's command with the promise, "Lord, from henceforth I will abide in Thee. " And when you set before yourself the life of love and joy, of holiness and fruitfulness, which in the future are to flow from abiding in Him, it is as if it only serves to make you still more hopeless: you, at least, can never attain to it. You know yourself too well. It is no use expecting it, only to be disappointed; a life fully and wholly abiding in Jesus is not for you.

—

Oh that you would learn a lesson from the time of your first coming to the Saviour! Remember, dear soul, how you then were led, contrary to all that your experience, and your feelings, and even your sober judgment said, to take Jesus at His word, and how you were not disappointed. He did receive you, and pardon you; He did love you, and save you -- you know it. And if He did this for you when you were an enemy and a stranger, what think you, now that you are His own, will He not much more fulfil His promise? Oh that you would come and begin simply to listen to His word, and to ask only the one question: Does He really mean that I should abide in Him? The answer His word gives is so simple and so sure: By His almighty grace you now are in Him; that same almighty grace will indeed enable you to abide in Him. By faith you became partakers of the initial grace; by that same faith you can enjoy the continuous grace of abiding in Him.

And if you ask what exactly it is that you now have to believe that you may abide in Him, the answer is not difficult. Believe first of all what He says: "I am the Vine." The safety and the fruitfulness of the branch depend upon the strength of the vine. Think not so much of yourself as a branch, nor of the abiding as your duty, until you have first had your soul filled with the faith of what Christ as the Vine is. He really will be to you all that a vine can be -- holding you fast, nourishing you, and making Himself every moment responsible for your growth and your fruit. Take time to know, set yourself heartily to believe: My Vine, on whom I can depend for all I need, is Christ. A large, strong vine bears the feeble branch, and holds it more than the branch holds the vine. Ask the Father by the Holy Ghost to reveal to you what a glorious, loving, mighty Christ this is, in whom you have your place and your life; it is the faith in what Christ is, more than anything else, that will keep you abiding in Him. A soul filled with large thoughts of the Vine will be a strong branch, and will abide confidently in Him. Be much occupied with Jesus, and believe much in Him, as the True Vine.

And then, when Faith can well say, "He is my Vine," let it further say, "I am His branch, I am in Him." I speak to those who say they are Christ's disciples, and on them I cannot too earnestly press the importance of exercising their faith in saying, "I am in Him." It makes the abiding so simple. If I realize clearly as I meditate: Now I am in Him, I see at once that there is nothing wanting but just my consent to be what He has made me, to remain where He has placed me. I am in Christ: This simple thought, carefully, prayerfully, believingly uttered, removes all difficulty as if there were some great attainment to be reached. No, I am in Christ, my blessed Saviour. His love has prepared a home for me with Himself, when He says, "Abide in my love"; and His power has undertaken to keep the door, and to keep me in, if I will but consent. I am in Christ: I have now but to say, "Saviour, I bless Thee for this wondrous grace. I consent; I yield myself to Thy gracious keeping; I do abide in Thee."

It is astonishing how such a faith will work out all that is further implied in abiding in Christ. There is in the Christian life great need of watchfulness and of prayer, of self-denial and of striving, of obedience and of diligence. But "all things are possible to him that believeth." "This is the victory that overcometh, even our faith." It is the faith that continually closes its eyes to the weakness of the creature, and finds its joy in the sufficiency of an Almighty Saviour, that makes the soul strong and glad. It gives itself up to be led by the Holy Spirit into an ever deeper appreciation of that wonderful Saviour whom God hath given us -- the Infinite Immanuel. It follows the leading of the Spirit from page to page of the blessed Word, with the one desire to take each revelation of what Jesus is and what He promises as its nourishment and its life. In accordance with the promise, "If that which ye have heard from the beginning abide in you, ye shall also abide in the Father and the Son," it lives by every word that proceedeth out of the mouth of God. And so it makes the soul strong with the strength of God, to be and to do all that is needed for abiding in Christ.

Believer, you would abide in Christ: only believe. Believe always; believe now. Bow even now before your Lord, and say to Him in childlike faith, that because He is your Vine, and you are His branch, you will this day abide in Him.

NOTE

" 'I am the True Vine.' He who offers us the privilege of an actual union with Himself is the great I AM, the almighty God, who upholds all things by the word of His power. And this almighty God reveals Himself as our perfect Saviour, even to the unimaginable extent of seeking to renew our fallen natures by grafting them into His own Divine nature.

"To realize the glorious Deity of Him whose call sounds forth to longing hearts with such exceeding sweetness, is no small step towards gaining the full privilege to which we are invited. But longing is by itself of no use; still less can there be any profit in reading of the blessed results to be gained from a close and personal union with our Lord, if we believe that union to be practically beyond our reach. His words are meant to be a living, an eternal, precious reality. And this they can never become unless we are sure that we may reasonably expect their accomplishment. But what could make the accomplishment of such an idea possible -- what could make it reasonable to suppose that we poor, weak, selfish creatures, full of sin and full of failures, might be saved out of the corruption of our nature and made partakers of the holiness of our Lord -- except the fact, the marvellous, unalterable fact, that He who proposes to us so great a transformation is Himself the everlasting God, as able as He is willing to fulfil His own word. In meditating, therefore, upon these utterances of Christ, containing as they do the very essence of His teaching, the very concentration of His love, let us, at the outset, put away all tendency to doubt. Let us not allow ourselves so much as to question whether such erring disciples as we are can be enabled to attain the holiness to which we are called through a close and intimate union with our Lord. If there be any impossibility, any falling short of the proposed blessedness, it will arise from the lack of earnest desire on our part. There is no lack in any respect on His part who puts forth the invitation; with GOD there can be no shortcoming in the fulfilment of His promise." -- The Life of Fellowship; Meditations on John 15:1,11 by A. M. James.

It is perhaps necessary to say, for the sake of young or doubting Christians, that there is something more necessary than the effort to exercise faith in each separate promise that is brought under our notice. What is of even greater importance is the cultivation of a trustful disposition towards God, the habit of always thinking of Him, of His ways and His works, with bright confiding hopefulness. In such soil alone can the individual promises strike root and grow up. In a little work published by the Tract Society, Encouragements to Faith, by James Kimball, there will be found many most suggestive and helpful thoughts, all pleading for the right God has to claim that He shall be trusted. The Christian's Secret of a Happy Life is another little work that has been a great help to many. Its bright and buoyant tone, its loving and unceasing repetition of the keynote -- we may indeed depend on Jesus to do all He has said, and more than we can think -- has breathed hope and joy into many a heart that was almost ready to despair of ever getting on. In Frances Havergal's Kept for the Master's Use, there is the same healthful, hope-inspiring tone.

Chapter 6 -- God Himself Has United You To Him

"OF GOD ARE YE IN CHRIST JESUS, who was made unto us wisdom from God, both righteousness and sanctification, and redemption." – 1 Cor.1:30 (R.V. marg.).
"My Father is the husbandman." -- John 15:1

"Ye ARE in Christ Jesus." The believers at Corinth were still feeble and carnal, only babes in Christ. And yet Paul wants them, at the outset of his teaching, to know distinctly that they are in Christ Jesus. The whole Christian life depends on the clear consciousness of our position in Christ. Most essential to the abiding in Christ is the daily renewal of our faith's assurance, "I am in Christ Jesus." All fruitful preaching to believers must take this as its starting point: "Ye are in Christ Jesus."

But the apostle has an additional thought, of almost greater importance: "OF GOD are ye in Christ Jesus." He would have us not only remember our union to Christ, but specially that it is not our own doing, but the work of God Himself. As the Holy Spirit teaches us to realize this, we shall see what a source of assurance and strength it must become to us. If it is of God alone that I am in Christ, then God Himself, the Infinite One, becomes my security for all I can need or wish in seeking to abide in Christ.

Let me try to understand what it means, this wonderful "OF GOD in Christ." In becoming partakers of the union with Christ, there is a work God does and a work we have to do. God does His work by moving us to do our work. The work of God is hidden and silent; what we do is something distinct and tangible. Conversion and faith, prayer and obedience, are conscious acts of which we can give a clear account; while the spiritual quickening and strengthening that come from above are secret and beyond the reach of human sight. And so it comes that when the believer tries to say, "I am in Christ Jesus," he looks more to the work he did, than to that wondrous secret work of God by which he was united to Christ. Nor can it well be otherwise at the commencement of the Christian course. "I know that I have believed," is a valid testimony. But it is of great consequence that the mind should be led to see that at the back of our turning, and believing, and accepting of Christ, there was God's almighty power doing its work -- inspiring our will, taking possession of us, and carrying out its own purpose of love in planting us into Christ Jesus. As the believer enters into this, the divine side of the work of salvation, he will learn to praise and to worship with new exultation, and to rejoice more than ever in the divineness of that salvation he has been made partaker of. At each step he reviews, the song will come, "This is the Lord's doing" -- Divine Omnipotence working out what Eternal Love had devised. "OF GOD I am in Christ Jesus."

The words will lead him even further and higher, even to the depths of eternity. "Whom He hath predestinated, them He also called." The calling in time is the manifestation of the purpose in eternity. Ere the world was, God had fixed the eye of His sovereign love on you in the election of grace, and chosen you in Christ. That you know yourself to be in Christ, is the stepping-stone by which you rise to understand in its full meaning the word, "OF GOD I am in Christ Jesus."

41

With the prophet, your language will be, "The Lord hath appeared of old unto me: yea, I have loved thee with an everlasting love, therefore with loving-kindness have I drawn thee." And you will recognise your own salvation as a part of that "mystery of His will, according to the good pleasure of His will which He purposed in Himself," and join with the whole body of believers in Christ as these say, "In whom we also have obtained an inheritance, being predestinated according to the purpose of Him who worketh all things after the counsel of His own will." Nothing will more exalt free grace, and make man bow very low before it, than this knowledge of the mystery "OF GOD in Christ."

It is easy to see what a mighty influence it must exert on the believer who seeks to abide in Christ. What a sure standing-ground it gives him, as he rests his right to Christ and all His fulness on nothing less than the Father's own purpose and work! We have thought of Christ as the Vine, and the believer as the branch; let us not forget that other precious word, "My Father is the husbandman." The Saviour said, "Every plant which my heavenly Father hath not planted, shall be rooted up"; but every branch grafted by Him in the True Vine, shall never be plucked out of His hand. As it was the Father to whom Christ owed all He was, and in whom He had all His strength and His life as the Vine, so to the Father the believer owes his place and his security in Christ. The same love and delight with which the Father watched over the beloved Son Himself, watch over every member of His body, every one who is in Christ Jesus.

—

What confident trust this faith inspires -- not only as to the being kept in safety to the end, but specially as to the being able to fulfil in every point the object for which I have been united to Christ. The branch is as much in the charge and keeping of the husbandman as the vine; his honour as much concerned in the wellbeing and growth of the branch as of the vine. The God who chose Christ to be Vine fitted Him thoroughly for the work He had as Vine to perform. The God who has chosen me and planted me in Christ, has thereby engaged to secure, if I will but let Him, by yielding myself to Him, that I in every way be worthy of Jesus Christ. Oh that I did but fully realize this! What confidence and urgency it would give to my prayer to the God and Father of Jesus Christ! How it would quicken the sense of dependence, and make me see that praying without ceasing is indeed the one need of my life -- an unceasing waiting, moment by moment, on the God who has united me to Christ, to perfect His own divine work, to work in me both to will and to do of His good pleasure.

And what a motive this would be for the highest activity in the maintenance of a fruitful branch-life! Motives are mighty powers; it is of infinite importance to have them high and clear. Here surely is the highest: "You are God's workmanship, created in Christ Jesus unto good works": grafted by Him into Christ, unto the bringing forth of much fruit. Whatever God creates is exquisitely suited to its end. He created the sun to give light: how perfectly it does its work! He created the eye to see: how beautifully it fulfils its object! He created the new man unto good works: how admirably it is fitted for its purpose.

OF GOD I am in Christ: created anew, made a branch of the Vine, fitted for fruit-bearing. Would to God that believers would cease looking most at their old nature, and complaining of their weakness, as if God called them to what they were unfitted for! Would that they would believingly and joyfully accept the wondrous revelation of how God, in uniting them to Christ, has made Himself chargeable for their spiritual growth and fruitfulness! How all sickly hesitancy and sloth would disappear, and under the influence of this mighty motive -- the faith in the faithfulness of Him of whom they are in Christ -- their whole nature would rise to accept and fulfil their glorious destiny!

O my soul! yield yourself to the mighty influence of this word: "OF GOD ye are in Christ Jesus." It is the same GOD OF WHOM Christ is made all that He is for us, OF WHOM we also are in Christ, and will most surely be made what we must be to Him. Take time to meditate and to worship, until the light that comes from the throne of God has shone into you, and you have seen your union to Christ as indeed the work of His almighty Father. Take time, day after day, and let, in your whole religious life, with all it has of claims and duties, of needs and wishes, God be everything. See Jesus, as He speaks to you, "Abide in me," pointing upward and saying, "My FATHER IS THE HUSBANDMAN. Of Him you are in me, through Him you abide in me, and to Him and to His glory shall be the fruit you bear." And let your answer be, Amen, Lord! So be it. From eternity Christ and I were ordained for each other; inseparably we belong to each other: it is God's will; I shall abide in Christ. It is of God I am in Christ Jesus.

Chapter 7 -- As Your Wisdom

"Of God are ye in Christ Jesus, who was made unto us WISDOM from God, both righteousness and sanctification, and redemption." – 1 Cor. 1:30 (R.V. marg.).

Jesus Christ is not only Priest to purchase, and King to secure, but also Prophet to reveal to us the salvation which God hath prepared for them that love Him. Just as at the creation the light was first called into existence, that in it all God's other works might have their life and beauty, so in our text wisdom is mentioned first as the treasury in which are to be found the three precious gifts that follow. The life is the light of man; it is in revealing to us, and making us behold the glory of God in His own face, that Christ makes us partakers of eternal life. It was by the tree of knowledge that sin came; it is through the knowledge that Christ gives that salvation comes. He is made of God unto us wisdom. In Him are hid all the treasures of wisdom and knowledge.

And of God you are in Him, and have but to abide in Him, to be made partaker of these treasures of wisdom. In Him you are, and in Him the wisdom is; dwelling in Him, you dwell in the very fountain of all light; abiding in Him, you have Christ the wisdom of God leading your whole spiritual life, and ready to communicate, in the form of knowledge, just as much as is needful for you to know. Christ is made unto us wisdom: you are in Christ.

It is this connection between what Christ has been made of God to us, and how we have it only as also being in Him, that we must learn to understand better. We shall thus see that the blessings prepared for us in Christ cannot be obtained as special gifts in answer to prayer apart from the abiding in Him. The answer to each prayer must come in the closer union and the deeper abiding in Him; in Him, the unspeakable gift, all other gifts are treasured up, the gift of wisdom and knowledge too.

How often have you longed for wisdom and spiritual understanding that you might know God better, whom to know is life eternal! Abide in Jesus: your life in Him will lead you to that fellowship with God in which the only true knowledge of God is to be had. His love, His power, His infinite glory will, as you abide in Jesus, be so revealed as it hath not entered into the heart of man to conceive. You may not be able to grasp it with the understanding, or to express it in words; but the knowledge which is deeper than thoughts or words will be given -- the knowing of God which comes of being known of Him. "We preach Christ crucified unto them which are called, Christ the power of God, and the wisdom of God."

Or you would fain count all things but loss for the excellency of the knowledge of Jesus Christ your Lord. Abide in Jesus, and be found in Him. You shall know Him in the power of His resurrection and the fellowship of His sufferings. Following Him, you shall not walk in darkness, but have the light of life. It is only when God shines into the heart, and Christ Jesus dwells there, that the light of the knowledge of God in the face of Christ can be seen.

—

Or would you understand his blessed work, as He wrought it on earth, or works it from heaven by His Spirit? Would you know how Christ can become our righteousness, and our sanctification, and redemption? It is just as bringing, and revealing, and communicating these that He is made unto us wisdom from God. There are a thousand questions that at times come up, and the attempt to answer them becomes a weariness and a burden. It is because you have forgotten you are in Christ, whom God has made to be your wisdom. Let it be your first care to abide in Him in undivided fervent devotion of heart; when the heart and the life are right, rooted in Christ, knowledge will come in such measure as Christ's own wisdom sees meet. And without such abiding in Christ the knowledge does not really profit, but is often most hurtful. The soul satisfies itself with thoughts which are but the forms and images of truth, without receiving the truth itself in its power. God's way is ever first to give us, even though it be but as a seed, the thing itself, the life and the power, and then the knowledge. Man seeks the knowledge first, and often, alas! never gets beyond it. God gives us Christ, and in Him hid the treasures of wisdom and knowledge. O let us be content to possess Christ, to dwell in Him, to make Him our life, and only in a deeper searching into Him, to search and find the knowledge we desire. Such knowledge is life indeed.

Therefore, believer, abide in Jesus as your wisdom, and expect from Him most confidently whatever teaching you may need for a life to the glory of the Father. In all that concerns your spiritual life, abide in Jesus as your wisdom. The life you have in Christ is a thing of infinite sacredness, far too high and holy for you to know how to act it out. It is He alone who can guide you, as by a secret spiritual instinct, to know what is becoming your dignity as a child of God, what will help and what will hinder your inner life, and specially your abiding in Him. Do not think of it as a mystery or a difficulty you must solve. Whatever questions come up as to the possibility of abiding perfectly and uninterruptedly in Him, and of really obtaining all the blessing that comes from it, always remember: He knows, all is perfectly clear to Him, and He is my wisdom. Just as much as you need to know and are capable of apprehending, will be communicated, if you only trust Him. Never think of the riches of wisdom and knowledge hid in Jesus as treasures without a key, or of your way as a path without a light. Jesus your wisdom is guiding you in the right way, even when you do not see it.

In all your intercourse with the blessed Word, remember the same truth: abide in Jesus, your wisdom. Study much to know the written Word; but study more to know the living Word, in whom you are of God. Jesus, the wisdom of God, is only known by a life of implicit confidence and obedience. The words He speaks are spirit and life to those who live in Him. Therefore, each time you read, or hear, or meditate upon the Word, be careful to take up your true position. Realize first your oneness with Him who is the wisdom of God; know yourself to be under His direct and special training; go to the Word abiding in Him, the very fountain of divine light -- in His light you shall see light.

In all your daily life, its ways and its work, abide in Jesus as your wisdom. Your body and your daily life share in the great salvation: in Christ, the wisdom of God, provision has been made for their guidance too. Your body is His temple, your daily life the sphere for glorifying Him: it is to Him a matter of deep interest that all your earthly concerns should be guided aright. Only trust His sympathy, believe His love, and wait for His guidance -- it will be given. Abiding in Him, the mind will be calmed and freed from passion, the judgment cleared and strengthened, the light of heaven will shine on earthly things, and your prayer for wisdom, like Solomon's, will be fulfilled above what you ask or think.

And so, especially in any work you do for God, abide in Jesus as your wisdom. "We are created in Christ Jesus unto good works, which God hath before ordained that we should walk in them"; let all fear or doubt lest we should not know exactly what these works are, be put far away. In Christ we are created for them: He will show us what they are, and how to do them. Cultivate the habit of rejoicing in the assurance that the divine wisdom is guiding you, even where you do not yet see the way.

All that you can wish to know is perfectly clear to Him. As Man, as Mediator, He has access to the counsels of Deity, to the secrets of Providence, in your interest, and on your behalf. If you will but trust Him fully, and abide in Him entirely, you can be confident of having unerring guidance.

Yes, abide in Jesus as your wisdom. Seek to maintain the spirit of waiting and dependence, that always seeks to learn, and will not move but as the heavenly light leads on. Withdraw yourself from all needless distraction, close your ears to the voices of the world, and be as a docile learner, ever listening for the heavenly wisdom the Master has to teach. Surrender all your own wisdom; seek a deep conviction of the utter blindness of the natural understanding in the things of God; and both as to what you have to believe and have to do, wait for Jesus to teach and to guide. Remember that the teaching and guidance come not from without: it is by His life in us that the divine wisdom does His work. Retire frequently with Him into the inner chamber of the heart, where the gentle voice of the Spirit is only heard if all be still. Hold fast with unshaken confidence, even in the midst of darkness and apparent desertion, His own assurance that He is the light and the leader of His own. And live, above all, day by day in the blessed truth that, as He Himself, the living Christ Jesus, is your wisdom, your first and last care must ever be this alone -- to abide in Him. Abiding in Him, His wisdom will come to you as the spontaneous outflowing of a life rooted in Him. I am, I abide in Christ, who was made unto us wisdom from God; wisdom will be given me.

Chapter 8 -- As Your Righteousness

"Of God are ye in Christ Jesus, who was made unto us wisdom from God, both RIGHTEOUSNESS and sanctification, and redemption."--1 Cor.1:30 (R.V. marg.).

The first of the great blessings which Christ our wisdom reveals to us as prepared in Himself, is -- righteousness. It is not difficult to see why this must be first.

There can be no real prosperity or progress in a nation, a home, or a soul, unless there be peace. As not even a machine can do its work unless it be in rest, secured on a good foundation, quietness and assurance are indispensable to our moral and spiritual well-being. Sin had disturbed all our relations; we were out of harmony with ourselves, with men, and with God. The first requirement of a salvation that should really bring blessedness to us was peace. And peace can only come with right. Where everything is as God would have it, in God's order and in harmony with His will, there alone can peace reign. Jesus Christ came to restore peace on earth, and peace in the soul, by restoring righteousness. Because He is Melchizedek, King of righteousness, He reigns as King of Salem, King of peace (Heb.7:2). He so fulfils the promise the prophets held out: "A king shall reign in righteousness: and the work of righteousness shall be peace, and the effect of righteousness, quietness and assurance for ever" (Isa.32:1,17). Christ is made of God unto us righteousness; of God we are in Him as our righteousness; we are made the righteousness of God in Him. Let us try to understand what this means.

When first the sinner is led to trust in Christ for salvation, he, as a rule, looks more to His work than His person.

As he looks at the Cross, and Christ suffering there, the Righteous One for the unrighteous, he sees in that atoning death the only but sufficient foundation for his faith in God's pardoning mercy. The substitution, and the curse-bearing, and the atonement of Christ dying in the stead of sinners, are what give him peace. And as he understands how the righteousness which Christ brings becomes his very own, and how, in the strength of that, he is counted righteous before God, he feels that he has what he needs to restore him to God's favour: "Being justified by faith, we have peace with God." He seeks to wear this robe of righteousness in the ever renewed faith in the glorious gift of righteousness which has been bestowed upon him.

—

But as time goes on, and he seeks to grow in the Christian life, new needs arise. He wants to understand more fully how it is that God can thus justify the ungodly on the strength of the righteousness of another. He finds the answer in the wonderful teaching of Scripture as to the true union of the believer with Christ as the second Adam. He sees that it is because Christ had made Himself one with His people, and they were one with Him; that it was in perfect accordance with all law in the kingdom of nature and of heaven, that each member of the body should have the full benefit of the doing and the suffering as of the life of the head. And so he is led to feel that it can only be in fully realizing his personal union with Christ as the Head, that he can fully experience the power of His righteousness to bring the soul into the full favour and fellowship of the Holy One. The work of Christ does not become less precious, but the Person of Christ more so; the work leads up into the very heart, the love and the life of the God-man.

And this experience sheds its light again upon Scripture. It leads him to notice, what he had scarce remarked before, how distinctly the righteousness of God, as it becomes ours, is connected with the Person of the Redeemer. "This is His name whereby HE shall be called, JEHOVAH OUR RIGHTEOUSNESS." "IN JEHOVAH have I righteousness and strength." "Of God is HE made unto us righteousness." "That we might be made the righteousness of God IN HIM." "That I may be found IN HIM, having the righteousness of God." He sees how inseparable righteousness and life in Christ are from each other: "The righteousness of one comes upon all unto justification of life." "They which receive the gift of righteousness shall reign in life by one, Jesus Christ." And he understands what deep meaning there is in the key-word of the Epistle to the Romans: "The righteous shall live by faith." He is not now content with only thinking of the imputed righteousness as his robe; but, putting on Jesus Christ, and seeking to be wrapped up in, to be clothed upon with Himself and His life, he feels how completely the righteousness of God is his, because the Lord our righteousness is his. Before he understood this, he too often felt it difficult to wear his white robe all the day: it was as if he specially had to put it on when he came into God's presence to confess his sins, and seek new grace. But now the living Christ Himself is his righteousness -- that Christ who watches over, and keeps and loves us as His own; it is no longer an impossibility to walk all the day enrobed in the loving presence with which He covers His people.

Such an experience leads still further. The life and the righteousness are inseparably linked, and the believer becomes more conscious than before of a righteous nature planted within him. The new man created in Christ Jesus, is "created in righteousness and true holiness." "He that doeth righteousness is righteous, even as He is righteous." The union to Jesus has effected a change not only in the relation to God, but in the personal state before God. And as the intimate fellowship to which the union has opened up the way is maintained, the growing renewal of the whole being makes righteousness to be his very nature.

—

To a Christian who begins to see the deep meaning of the truth, "HE is made to us righteousness," it is hardly necessary to say, "Abide in Him." As long as he only thought of the righteousness of the substitute, and our being counted judicially righteous for His sake, the absolute necessity of abiding in Him was not apparent. But as the glory of "Jehovah our righteousness" unfolds to the view, he sees that abiding in Him personally is the only way to stand, at all times, complete and accepted before God, as it is the only way to realize how the new and righteous nature can be strengthened from Jesus our Head. To the penitent sinner the chief thought was the righteousness which comes through Jesus dying for sin; to the intelligent and advancing believer, Jesus, the Living One, through whom the righteousness comes, is everything, because having Him he has the righteousness too.

Believer, abide in Christ as your righteousness. You bear about with you a nature altogether corrupt and vile, ever seeking to rise up and darken your sense of acceptance, and of access to unbroken fellowship with the Father. Nothing can enable you to dwell and walk in the light of God, without even the shadow of a cloud between, but the habitual abiding in Christ as your righteousness. To this you are called. Seek to walk worthy of that calling. Yield yourself to the Holy Spirit to reveal to you the wonderful grace that permits you to draw nigh to God, clothed in a divine righteousness. Take time to realize that the King's own robe has indeed been put on, and that in it you need not fear entering His presence. It is the token that you are the man whom the King delights to honour. Take time to remember that as much as you need it in the palace, no less do you require it when He sends you forth into the world, where you are the King's messenger and representative. Live your daily life in the full consciousness of being righteous in God's sight, an object of delight and pleasure in Christ. Connect every view you have of Christ in His other graces with this first one: "Of God He is made to you righteousness." This will keep you in perfect peace. Thus shall you enter into, and dwell in, the rest of God. So shall your inmost being be transformed into being righteous and doing righteousness. In your heart and life it will become manifest where you dwell; abiding in Jesus Christ, the Righteous One, you will share His position, His character, and His blessedness: "Thou lovest righteousness, and hatest iniquity: therefore God, thy God, hath anointed thee with the oil of gladness above thy fellows." Joy and gladness above measure will be your portion.

Chapter 9 -- As Your Sanctification

"Of God are ye in Christ Jesus, who has made unto us wisdom from God, both righteousness and SANCTIFICATION, and redemption." – 1 Cor.1:30(R.V. marg.).

"Paul, unto the Church of God which is at Corinth to them that are sanctified in Christ Jesus, called to be saints"; -- thus the chapter opens in which we are taught that Christ is our sanctification. In the Old Testament, believers were called the righteous; in the New Testament they are called saints, the holy ones, sanctified in Christ Jesus. Holy is higher than righteous.[1] Holy in God has reference to His inmost being; righteous, to His dealings with His creatures. In man, righteousness is but a tepping-stone to holiness. It is in this he can approach most near to the perfection of God (comp. Matt.5:48; I Pet.1:16). In the Old Testament righteousness was found, while holiness was only typified; in Jesus Christ, the Holy One, and in His people, His saints or holy ones, it is first realized.

As in Scripture, and in our text, so in personal experience righteousness precedes holiness. When first the believer finds Christ as his righteousness, he has such joy in the new-made discovery that the study of holiness hardly has a place. But as he grows, the desire for holiness makes itself felt, and he seeks to know what provision his God has made for supplying that need. A superficial acquaintance with God's plan leads to the view that while justification is God's work, by faith in Christ, sanctification is our work, to be performed under the influence of the gratitude we feel for the deliverance we have experienced, and by the aid of the Holy Spirit. But the earnest Christian soon finds how little gratitude can supply the power. When he thinks that more prayer will bring it, he finds that, indispensable as prayer is, it is not enough. Often the believer struggles hopelessly for years, until he listens to the teaching of the Spirit, as He glorifies Christ again, and reveals Christ, our anctification, to be appropriated by faith alone.

Christ is made of God unto us sanctification. Holiness is the very nature of God, and that alone is holy which God takes possession of and fills with Himself. God's answer to the question, How could sinful man become holy? is, "Christ, the Holy One of God." In Him, whom the Father sanctified and sent into the world, God's holiness was revealed incarnate, and brought within reach of man. "I sanctify myself for them, that they also may be sanctified in truth." There is no other way of our becoming holy, but by becoming partakers of the holiness of Christ. [2] And there is no other way of this taking place than by our personal spiritual union with Him, so that through His Holy Spirit His holy life flows into us. "Of God are ye in Christ, who is made unto us sanctification." Abiding by faith in Christ our sanctification is the simple secret of a holy life. The measure of sanctification will depend on the measure of abiding in Him; as the soul learns wholly to abide in Christ, the promise is increasingly fulfilled: "The very God of peace sanctify you wholly."

58

To illustrate this relation between the measure of the abiding and the measure of sanctification experienced,let us think of the grafting a tree, that instructive symbol of our union to Jesus. The illustration is suggested by the Saviour's words, "Make the tree good, and his fruit good." I can graft a tree so that only a single branch bears good fruit, while many of the natural branches remain, and bear their old fruit -- a type of believer in whom a small part of the life is sanctified, but in whom, from ignorance or other reasons, the carnal life still in many respects has full dominion. I can graft a tree so that every branch is cut off, and the whole tree becomes renewed to bear good fruit; and yet, unless I watch over the tendency of the stems to give sprouts, they may again rise and grow strong, and, robbing the new graft of the strength it needs, make it weak. Such are Christians who, when apparently powerfully converted, forsake all to follow Christ, and yet after a time, through unwatchfulness, allow old habits to regain their power, and whose Christian life and fruit are but feeble. But if I want a tree wholly made good, I take it when young, and, cutting the stem clean off on the ground, I graft it just where it emerges from the soil. I watch over every bud which the old nature could possibly put forth, until the flow of sap from the old roots into the new stem is so complete, that the old life has, as it were, been entirely conquered and covered by the new. Here I have a tree entirely renewed -- emblem of the Christian who has learnt in entire consecration to surrender everything for Christ, and in a whole-hearted faith wholly to abide in Him.

If, in this last case, the old tree were a reasonable being that could co-operate with the gardener, what would his language be to it? Would it not be this: "Yield now yourself entirely to this new nature with which I have invested you; repress every tendency of the old nature to give buds or sprouts; let all your sap and all your life-powers rise up into this graft from yonder beautiful tree, which I have put on you; so shall you bring forth sweet and much fruit." And the language of the tree to the gardener would be: "When you graft me, O spare not a single branch; let everything of the old self, even the smallest bud, be destroyed, that I may no longer live in my own, but in that other life that was cut off and brought and put upon me, that I might be wholly new and good." And, once again, could you afterwards ask the renewed tree, as it was bearing abundant fruit, what it could say of itself, its answer would be this: "In me, that is, in my roots, there dwells no good thing. I am ever inclined to evil; the sap I collect from the soil is in its nature corrupt, and ready to show itself in bearing evil fruit. But just when the sap rises into the sunshine to ripen into fruit, the wise gardener has clothed me with a new life, through which my sap is purified, and all my powers are renewed to the bringing forth of good fruit. I have only to abide in that which I have received. He cares for the immediate repression and removal of every bud which the old nature still would put forth."

Christian, fear not to claim God's promises to make you holy. Listen not to the suggestion that the corruption of your old nature would render holiness an impossibility. In your flesh dwells no good thing, and that flesh, though crucified with Christ, is not yet dead, but will continually seek to rise and lead you to evil. But the Father is the Husbandman. He has grafted the life of Christ on your life. That holy life is mightier than your evil life; under the watchful care of the Husbandman, that new life can keep down the workings of the evil life within you. The evil nature is there, with its unchanged tendency to rise up and show itself. But the new nature is there too -- the living Christ, your sanctification, is there -- and through Him all your powers can be sanctified as they rise into life, and be made to bear fruit to the glory of the Father.

And now, if you would live a holy life, abide in Christ your sanctification. Look upon Him as the Holy One of God, made man that He might communicate to us the holiness of God. Listen when Scripture teaches that there is within you a new nature, a new man, created in Christ Jesus in righteousness and true holiness. Remember that this holy nature which is in you is singularly fitted for living a holy life, and performing all holy duties, as much so as the old nature is for doing evil. Understand that this holy nature within you has its root and life in Christ in heaven, and can only grow and become strong as the intercourse between it and its source is uninterrupted. And above all, believe most confidently that Jesus Christ Himself delights in maintaining that new nature within you, and imparting to it His own strength and wisdom for its work. Let that faith lead you daily to the surrender of all self-confidence, and the confession of the utter corruption of all there is in you by nature. Let it fill you with a quiet and assured confidence that you are indeed able to do what the Father expects of you as His child, under the covenant of His grace, because you have Christ strengthening you. Let it teach you to lay yourself and your services on the altar as spiritual sacrifices, holy and acceptable in His sight, a sweet-smelling savour. Look not upon a life of holiness as a strain and an effort, but as the natural outgrowth of the life of Christ within you. And let ever again a quiet, hopeful, gladsome faith hold itself assured that all you need for a holy life will most assuredly be given you out of the holiness of Jesus. Thus will you understand and prove what it is to abide in Christ our sanctification.

NOTE

The thought that in the personal holiness of our Lord a new holy nature was formed to be communicated to us, and that we make use of it by faith, is the central idea of Marshall's invaluable work, The Gospel Mystery of Sanctcation:

"One great mystery is, that the holy frame and disposition whereby our souls are furnished and enabled for immediate practice of the law, must be obtained by receiving it out of Christ's fulness, as a thing already prepared and brought to an existence for us in Christ, and treasured up in Him; and that, as we are justified by a righteousness wrought out in Christ, and imputed to us, so we are sanctified by such an holy frame and qualification as are first wrought out and completed in Christ for us, and then imparted to us. As our natural corruption was produced originally in the first Adam, and propagated from him to us, so our new nature and holiness is first produced in Christ, and derived from Him to us, or, as it were, propagated. So that we are not at all to work together with Christ in making or producing that holy frame in us, but only to take it to ourselves, and use it in our holy practice, as made ready to our hands. Thus we have fellowship with Christ, in receiving that holy frame of spirit that was originally in Him; for fellowship is where several persons have the same things in common. This mystery is so great, that notwithstanding all the light of the Gospel, we commonly think that we must get an holy frame by producing it anew in ourselves, and by pursuing it and working it out of our own heart" (see chap. 3). [3]

Footnotes:

1. "Holiness may be called spiritual perection, as righteousnes is legal completeness." -- Horatius Bonar in God's Way of Holiness.

2. See note at end of chapter.

---

3. I have felt so strongly that the teaching of Marshall is just what the Church needs to bring out clearly what the Scripture path of holiness is, that I have prepared an abridgment (all in the author's own words) of his work. By leaving out what was not essential to his argument, and shortening when he appeared diffuse, I hoped to bring his book within reach of many who might never read the larger work. It is published by Nisbet & Co. under the title, The Highway of Holiness. I cannot too earnestly urge every student of theology, and of Scripture, and of the art of holy living, to make himself master of the teaching of Marshall's third, fourth, and twelfth chapters.

Publisher's Note: The original complete work, The Gospel Mystery of Sanctification, was reissued by Oliphants Ltd. in 1955.

Chapter 10 -- As Your Redemption

"Of God are ye in Christ Jesus, who was made unto us wisdom from God, both righteousness and sanctification, and REDEMPTION." -- 1 Cor.1:30(R.V. marg.).

Here we have the top of the ladder, reaching into heaven --
the blessed end to which Christ and life in Him is to lead. The
word redemption, though sometimes applied to our
deliverance from the guilt of sin, here refers to our complete
and final deliverance from all its consequences, when the
Redeemer's work shall become fully manifest, even to the
redemption of the body itself (comp. Rom.8:21-23; Eph.1.14;
4:30). The expression points us to the highest glory to be
hoped for in the future, and therefore also to the highest
blessing to be enjoyed in the present in Christ. We have seen
how, as a Prophet, Christ is our wisdom, revealing to us God
and His love, with the nature and conditions of the salvation
that love has prepared. As a Priest, He is our righteousness,
restoring us to right relations to God, and securing us His
favour and friendship. As a King, He is our sanctification,
forming and guiding us into the obedience to the Father's holy
will. As these three offices work out God's one purpose, the
grand consummation will be reached,the complete deliverance
from sin and all its effects be accomplished, and ransomed
humanity regain all that it had ever lost.

Christ is made of God unto us redemption. The word invites us
to look upon Jesus, not only as He lived on earth, teaching us
by word and example, as He died, to reconcile us with God, as
He lives again, a victorious King, rising to receive His crown,
but as, sitting at the right hand of God, He takes again the
glory which He had with the Father, before the world began,
and holds it there for us. It consists in this, that there His
human nature, yea, His human body, freed from all the
consequences of sin to which He once had been exposed, is
now admitted to share the divine glory. As Son of Man, He
dwells on the throne and in the bosom of the Father: the
deliverance from what He had to suffer from sin is complete
and eternal. The complete redemption is found embodied in
His own Person: what He as man is and has in heaven is the
complete redemption. HE is made of God to us redemption.

We are in Him as such. And the more intelligently and believingly we abide in Him as our redemption, the more shall we experience, even here, of "the powers of the world to come." As our communion with Him becomes more intimate and intense, and we let the Holy Spirit reveal Him to us in His heavenly glory, the more we realize how the life in us is the life of One who sits upon the throne of heaven. We feel the power of an endless life working in us. We taste the eternal life. We have the foretaste of the eternal glory.

The blessings flowing from abiding in Christ as our redemption are great. The soul is delivered from all fear of death. There was a time when even the Saviour feared death. But now no longer. He has triumphed over death; even His body has entered into the glory. The believer who abides in Christ as his full redemption, realizes even now his spiritual victory over death. It becomes to him the servant that removes the last rags of the old carnal vesture, ere he be clothed upon with the new body of glory. It carries the body to the grave, to lie there as the seed whence the new body will arise the worthy companion of the glorified spirit. The resurrection of the body is no longer a barren doctrine, but a living expectation, and even an incipient experience, because the Spirit of Him that raised Jesus from the dead, dwells in the body as the pledge that even our mortal bodies shall be quickened (Rom.8:11-23). This faith exercises its sanctifying influence in the willing surrender of the sinful members of the body to be mortified and completely subjected to the dominion of the Spirit, as preparation for the time when the frail body shall be changed and fashioned like to His glorious body.

This full redemption of Christ as extending to the body, has a depth of meaning not easily expressed. It was of man as a whole, soul and body that it is said that he was made in the image and likeness of God. In the angels, God had created spirits without material bodies; in the creation of the world, there was matter without spirit. Man was to be the highest specimen of divine art: the combination in one being, of matter and spirit in perfect harmony, as type of the most perfect union between God and His own creation. Sin entered in, and appeared to thwart the divine plan: the material obtained a fearful supremacy over the spiritual. The Word was made flesh, the divine fulness received an embodiment in the humanity of Christ, that the redemption might be a complete and perfect one; that the whole creation, which now groaneth and travaileth in pain together, might be delivered from the bondage of corruption into the liberty of the glory of the children of God. God's purpose will not be accomplished, and Christ's glory will not be manifested fully, until the body, with that whole of nature of which it is part and head, has been transfigured by the power of the spiritual life, and made the transparent vesture for showing forth the glory of the Infinite Spirit. Then only shall we understand: "Christ Jesus is made unto us (complete) redemption."

Meantime we are taught to believe: "Of God are ye in Christ, as your redemption." This is not meant as a revelation, to be left to the future; for the full development of the Christian life, our present abiding in Christ must seek to enter into and appropriate it. We do this as we learn to triumph over death. We do it as we learn to look upon Christ as the Lord of our body, claiming its entire consecration, securing even here, if faith will claim it (Mark 16:17-18), victory over the terrible dominion sin hath had in the body. We do this as we learn to look on all nature as part of the Kingdom of Christ, destined, even though it be through a baptism of fire, to partake in His redemption. We do it as we allow the powers of the coming world to possess us, and to lift us up into a life in the heavenly places, to enlarge our hearts and our views, to anticipate, even here, the things which have never entered into the heart of man to conceive.

—

Believer, abide in Christ as your redemption. Let this be the crown of your Christian life. Seek it not first or only, apart from the knowledge of Christ in His other relations. But seek it truly as that to which they are meant to lead you up. Abide in Christ as your redemption. Nothing will fit you for this but faithfulness in the previous steps of the Christian life. Abide in Him as your wisdom, the perfect revelation of all that God is and has for you. Follow, in the daily ordering of the inner and the outer life, with meek docility His teaching, and you shall be counted worthy to have secrets revealed to you which to most disciples are a sealed book. The wisdom will lead you into the mysteries of complete redemption. Abide in Him as your righteousness, and dwell clothed upon with Him in that inner sanctuary of the Father's favour and presence to which His righteousness gives you access. As you rejoice in your reconciliation, you shall understand how it includes all things, and how they too wait the full redemption; "for it pleased the Father by Him to reconcile all things unto Himself; by Him, I say, whether they be things on earth or things in heaven." And abide in Him as your sanctification; the experience of His power to make you holy, spirit and soul and body, will quicken your faith in a holiness that shall not cease its work until the bells of the horses and every pot in Jerusalem shall be holiness to the Lord. Abide in Him as your redemption, and live, even here, as the heir of the future glory. And as you seek to experience in yourself to the full, the power of His saving grace, your heart shall be enlarged to realize the position man has been destined to occupy in the universe, as having all things made subject to him, and you shall for your part be fitted to live worthy of that high and heavenly calling.

Chapter 11 -- The Crucified One

"I am crucified with Christ: nevertheless I live; yet not I, but Christ liveth in me." -- Gal.2:20.
"We have been planted together in the likeness of his death. " -- Rom.6:5

"I am crucified with Christ." Thus the apostle expresses his assurance of his fellowship with Christ in His sufferings and death, and his full participation in all the power and the blessing of that death. And so really did he mean what he said, and know that he was now indeed dead, that he adds: "It is no longer I that live, but Christ that liveth in me."How blessed must be the experience of such a union with the Lord Jesus! To be able to look upon His death as mine, just as really as it was His -- upon His perfect obedience to God, His victory over sin, and complete deliverance from its power, as mine; and to realize that the power of that death does by faith work daily with a divine energy in mortifying the flesh, and renewing the whole life into the perfect conformity to the resurrection life of Jesus! Abiding in Jesus, the Crucified One, is the secret of the growth of that new life which is ever begotten of the death of nature.

Let us try to understand this. The suggestive expression, "Planted into the likeness of His death," will teach us what the abiding in the Crucified One means. When a graft is united with the stock on which it is to grow, we know that it must be kept fixed, it must abide in the place where the stock has been cut, been wounded, to make an opening to receive the graft. No graft without wounding -- the laying bare and opening up of the inner life of the tree to receive the stranger branch. It is only through such wounding that access can be obtained to the fellowship of the sap and the growth and the life of the stronger stem. Even so with Jesus and the sinner. Only when we are planted into the likeness of His death shall we also be in the likeness of His resurrection, partakers of the life and the power there are in Him. In the death of the Cross Christ was wounded, and in His opened wounds a place prepared where we might be grafted in. And just as one might say to a graft, and does practically say as it is fixed in its place, "Abide here in the wound of the stem, that is now to bear you"; so to the believing soul the message comes, "Abide in the wounds of Jesus; there is the place of union, and life, and growth. There you shall see how His heart was opened to receive you; how His flesh was rent that the way might be opened for your being made one with Him, and having access to all the blessings flowing from His divine nature."

You have also noticed how the graft has to be torn away from the tree where it by nature grew, and to be cut into conformity to the place prepared for it in the wounded stem. Even so the believer has to be made conformable to Christ's death -- to be crucified and to die with Him. The wounded stem and the wounded graft are cut to fit into each other, into each other's likeness. There is a fellowship between Christ's sufferings and your sufferings. His experiences must become yours. The disposition He manifested in choosing and bearing the cross must be yours. Like Him, you will have to give full assent to the righteous judgment and curse of a holy God against sin. Like Him, you have to consent to yield your life, as laden with sin and curse,to death, and through it to pass to the new life. Like Him, you shall experience that it is only through the self-sacrifice of Gethsemane and Calvary that the path is to be found to the joy and the fruit-bearing of the resurrection life. The more clear the resemblance between the wounded stem and the wounded graft, the more exactly their wounds fit into each other, the surer and the easier, and the more complete will be the union and the growth.

It is in Jesus, the Crucified One, I must abide. I must learn to look upon the Cross as not only an atonement to God, but also a victory over the devil -- not only a deliverance from the guilt, but also from the power of sin. I must gaze on Him on the Cross as wholly mine, offering Himself to receive me into the closest union and fellowship, and to make me partaker of the full power of His death to sin, and the new life of victory to which it is but the gateway. I must yield myself to Him in an undivided surrender, with much prayer and strong desire, imploring to be admitted into the ever closer fellowship and conformity of His death, of the Spirit in which He died that death.

71

Let me try and understand why the Cross is thus the place of union. On the Cross the Son of God enters into the fullest union with man -- enters into the fullest experience of what it says to have become a son of man, a member of a race under the curse. It is in death that the Prince of life conquers the power of death; it is in death alone that He can make me partaker of that victory. The life He imparts is a life from the dead; each new experience of the power of that life depends upon the fellowship of the death. The death and the life are inseparable. All the grace which Jesus the Saving One gives is given only in the path of fellowship with Jesus the Crucified One. Christ came and took my place; I must put myself in His place, and abide there. And there is but one place which is both His and mine -- that place is the Cross. His in virtue of His free choice; mine by reason of the curse of sin. He came there to seek me; there alone I can find Him. When He found me there, it was the place of cursing; this He experienced, for "cursed is every one that hangeth on a tree." He made it a place of blessing; this I experienced, for Christ has delivered us from the curse, being made a curse for us. When Christ comes in my place, He remains what He was, the beloved of the Father; but in the fellowship with me He shares my curse and dies my death. When I stand in His place, which is still always mine, I am still what I was by nature, the accursed one, who deserves to die; but as united to Him, I share His blessing, and receive His life. When He came to be one with me He could not avoid the Cross, for the curse always points to the Cross as its end and fruit. And when I seek to be one with Him, I cannot avoid the Cross either, for nowhere but on the Cross are life and deliverance to be found. As inevitably as my curse pointed Him to the Cross as the only place where He could be fully united to me, His blessing points me to the Cross too as the only place where I can be united to Him. He took my cross for His own; I must take His Cross as my own; I must be crucified with Him. It is as I abide daily, deeply in Jesus the Crucified One, that I shall taste the sweetness of His love, the power of His life, the completeness of His salvation.

Beloved believer! it is a deep mystery, this of the Cross of Christ. I fear there are many Christians who are content to look upon the Cross, with Christ on it dying for their sins, who have little heart for fellowship with the Crucified One. They hardly know that He invites them to it. Or they are content to consider the ordinary afflictions of life, which the children of the world often have as much as they, as their share of Christ's Cross. They have no conception of what it is to be crucified with Christ, that bearing the cross means likeness to Christ in the principles which animated Him in His path of obedience. The entire surrender of all self-will, the complete denial to the flesh of its every desire and pleasure, the perfect separation from the world in all its ways of thinking and acting, the losing and hating of one's life, the giving up of self and its interests for the sake of others -- this is the disposition which marks him who has taken up Christ's Cross, who seeks to say, "I am crucified with Christ; I abide in Christ, the Crucified One."

Would you in very deed please your Lord, and live in as close fellowship with Him as His grace could maintain you in? O pray that His Spirit lead you into this blessed truth: this secret of the Lord for them that fear Him. We know how Peter knew and confessed Christ as the Son of the living God while the Cross was still an offence (Matt.16:16,17,21,23). The faith that believes in the blood that pardons, and the life that renews, can only reach its perfect growth as it abides beneath the Cross, and in living fellowship with Him seeks for perfect conformity with Jesus the Crucified.

O Jesus, our crucified Redeemer, teach us not only to believe on Thee, but to abide in Thee, to take Thy Cross not only as the ground of our pardon, but also as the law of our life. O teach us to love it not only because on it Thou didst bear our curse, but because on it we enter into the closest fellowship with Thyself, and are crucified with Thee. And teach us, that as we yield ourselves wholly to be possessed of the Spirit in which Thou didst bear the Cross, we shall be made partakers of the power and the blessing to which the Cross alone gives access.

Chapter 12 -- God Himself Will Stablish You In Him

"He which stablisheth us with you in Christ, is God."-- 2 Cor.1:21

These words of Paul teach us a much needed and most blessed truth -- that just as our first being united with Christ was the work of divine omnipotence, so we may look to the Father, too, for being kept and being fixed more firmly in Him. "The Lord will perfect that which concerneth me" -- this expression of confidence should ever accompany the prayer, "Forsake not the work of Thine own hands." In all his longings and prayers to attain to a deeper and more perfect abiding in Christ, the believer must hold fast his confidence: "He which hath begun a good work in you, will perform it until the day of Jesus Christ." There is nothing that will so help to root and ground him in Christ as this faith: "He which stablisheth us in Christ is God."

How many there are who can witness that this faith is just what they need! They continually mourn over the variableness of their spiritual life. Sometimes there are hours and days of deep earnestness, and even of blessed experience of the grace of God. But how little is needed to mar their peace, to bring a cloud over the soul! And then, how their faith is shaken! All efforts to regain their standing appear utterly fruitless; and neither solemn vows, nor watching and prayer, avail to restore to them the peace they for a while had tasted. Could they but understand how just their own efforts are the cause of their failure, because it is God alone who can establish us in Christ Jesus. They would see that just as in justification they had to cease from their own working, and to accept in faith the promise that God would give them life in Christ, so now, in the matter of their sanctification, their first need is to cease from striving themselves to establish the connection with Christ more firmly, and to allow God to do it. "God is faithful, by whom ye were called unto the fellowship of His Son Jesus Christ." What they need is the simple faith that the stablishing in Christ, day by day, is God's work -- a work that He delights to do, in spite of all our weakness and unfaithfulness, if we will but trust Him for it.

To the blessedness of such a faith, and the experience it brings, many can testify. What peace and rest, to know that there is a Husbandman who cares for the branch, to see that it grows stronger, and that its union with the Vine becomes more perfect, who watches over every hindrance and danger, who supplies every needed aid! What peace and rest, fully and finally to give up our abiding into the care of God, and never have a wish or thought, never to offer a prayer or engage in an exercise connected with it, without first having the glad remembrance that what we do is only the manifestation of what God is doing in us! The establishing in Christ is His work: He accomplishes it by stirring us to watch, and wait, and work. But this He can do with power only as we cease interrupting Him by our self-working -- as we accept in faith the dependent posture which honours Him and opens the heart to let Him work. How such a faith frees the soul from care and responsibility! In the midst of the rush and bustle of the world's stirring life, amid the subtle and ceaseless temptations of sin, amid all the daily cares and trials that so easily distract and lead to failure, how blessed it would be to be an established Christian -- always abiding in Christ! How blessed even to have the faith that one can surely become it -- that the attainment is within our reach!

Dear believer, the blessing is indeed within your reach. He that stablisheth you with us in Christ is God. What I want you to take in is this -- that believing this promise will not only give you comfort, but will be the means of your obtaining your desire. You know how Scripture teaches us that in all God's leadings of His people faith has everywhere been the one condition of the manifestation of His power. Faith is the ceasing from all nature's efforts, and all other dependence; faith is confessed helplessness casting itself upon God's promise, and claiming its fulfilment; faith is the putting ourselves quietly into God's hands for Him to do His work. What you and I need now is to take time, until this truth stands out before us in all its spiritual brightness: It is God Almighty, God the Faithful and Gracious One, who has undertaken to stablish me in Christ Jesus.

—

Listen to what the Word teaches you: -- "The Lord shall establish thee an holy people unto Himself"; "O Lord God, stablish their heart unto Thee"; "Thy God loved Israel, to establish them for ever"; "Thou wilt establish the heart of the humble"; "Now to Him that is of power to establish you, be glory for ever"; "To the end He may establish your hearts unblameable in holiness" ; "THE LORD IS FAITHFUL, who shall stablish you and keep you from all evil"; "The God of all grace, who hath called us in Christ Jesus, make you perfect, stablish, strengthen, settle you." Can you take these words to mean anything less than that you too -- however fitful your spiritual life has hitherto been, however unfavourable your natural character or your circumstances may appear -- can be established in Christ Jesus -- can become an established Christian? Let us but take time to listen, in simple childlike teachableness, to these words as the truth of God, and the confidence will come: As surely -- as I am in Christ, I shall also, day by day, be established in Him.

The lesson appears so simple; and yet the most of us take so long to learn it. The chief reason is, that the grace the promise offers is so large, so God-like, so beyond all our thoughts, that we do not take it really to mean what it says. The believer who has once come to see and accept what it brings, can bear witness to the wonderful change there comes over the spiritual life. Hitherto he had taken charge of his own welfare; now he has a God to take charge of it. He now knows himself to be in the school of God, a Teacher who plans the whole course of study for each of His pupils with infinite wisdom, and delights to have them come daily for the lessons He has to give. All he asks is to feel himself constantly in God's hands, and to follow His guidance, neither lagging behind nor going before. Remembering that it is God who worketh both to will and to do, he sees his only safety to be in yielding himself to God's working. He lays aside all anxiety about his inner life and its growth, because the Father is the Husbandman under whose wise and watchful care each plant is well secured. He knows that there is the prospect of a most blessed life of strength and fruitfulness to every one who will take God alone and wholly as his hope.

Believer, you cannot but admit that such a life of trust must be a most blessed one. You say, perhaps, that there are times when you do, with your whole heart, consent to this way of living, and do wholly abandon the care of your inner life to your Father. But somehow it does not last. You forget again; and instead of beginning each morning with the joyous transference of all the needs and cares of your spiritual life to the Father's charge, you again feel anxious, and burdened, and helpless. Is it not, perhaps, my brother, because you have not committed to the Father's care this matter of daily remembering to renew your entire surrender? Memory is one of the highest powers in our nature. By it day is linked to day, the unity of life through all our years is kept up, and we know that we are still ourselves. In the spiritual life, recollection is of infinite value. For the sanctifying of our memory, in the service of our spiritual life, God has provided most beautifully. The Holy Spirit is the remembrancer, the Spirit of recollection. Jesus said, "He shall bring all things to your remembrance." "He which stablisheth us with you in Christ is God, who hath also sealed us, and given the earnest of the Spirit in our hearts." It is just for the stablishing that the Holy Remembrancer has been given. God's blessed promises, and your unceasing acts of faith and surrender accepting of them -- He will enable you to remember these each day. The Holy Spirit is -- blessed be God -- the memory of the new man.

Apply this to the promise of the text: "He that stablisheth us in Christ is God." As you now, at this moment, abandon all anxiety about your growth and progress to the God who has undertaken to stablish you in the Vine, and feel what a joy it is to know that God alone has charge, ask and trust Him by the Holy Spirit ever to remind you of this your blessed relation to Him. He will do it; and with each new morning your faith may grow stronger and brighter: I have a God to see that each day I become more firmly united to Christ.

And now, beloved fellow-believer, "the God of all grace, who hath called us in Christ Jesus, make you perfect, stablish, strengthen, settle you." What more can you desire? Expect it confidently, ask it fervently. Count on God to do His work. And learn in faith to sing the song, the notes of which each new experience will make deeper and sweeter: "Now to Him, that is of power to establish you, be glory for ever. Amen." Yes, glory to God, who has undertaken to establish us in Christ!

Chapter 13 -- Every Moment

"In that day sing ye unto her, A vineyard of red wine. I the Lord do keep it; I will water it every moment: lest any hurt it, I will keep it night and day." -- Isa.27:2,3.

The vineyard was the symbol of the people of Israel, in whose midst the True Vine was to stand. The branch is the symbol of the individual believer, who stands in the Vine. The song of the vineyard is also the song of the Vine and its every branch. The command still goes forth to the watchers of the vineyard -- would that they obeyed it, and sang till every feeble-hearted believer had learned and joined the joyful strain -- "Sing ye unto her: I, JEHOVAH, Do KEEP IT; I will water it every moment: lest any hurt it, I WILL KEEP it night and day."

What an answer from the mouth of God Himself to the question so often asked: Is it possible for the believer always to abide in Jesus? Is a life of unbroken fellowship with the Son of God indeed attainable here in this earthly life? Truly not, if the abiding is our work, to be done in our strength. But the things that are impossible with men are possible with God. If the Lord Himself will keep the soul night and day, yea, will watch and water it every moment, then surely the uninterrupted communion with Jesus becomes a blessed possibility to those who can trust God to mean and to do what He says. Then surely the abiding of the branch of the vine day and night, summer and winter, in a never-ceasing life-fellowship, is nothing less than the simple but certain promise of your abiding in your Lord.

In one sense, it is true, there is no believer who does not always abide in Jesus; without this there could not be true life. "If a man abide not in me, he is cast forth." But when the Saviour gives the command, "Abide in me," with the promise, "He that abideth in me bringeth forth much fruit," He speaks of that willing, intelligent, and whole-hearted surrender by which we accept His offer, and consent to the abiding in Him as the only life we choose or seek. The objections raised against our right to expect that we shall always be able thus voluntarily and consciously to abide in Jesus are chiefly two.

The one is derived from the nature of man. It is said that our limited powers prevent our being occupied with two things at the same moment. God's providence places many Christians in business, where for hours at a time the closest attention is required to the work they have to do. How can such a man, it is asked, with his whole mind in the work he has to do, be at the same time occupied with Christ, and keeping up fellowship with Him? The consciousness of abiding in Jesus is regarded as requiring such a strain, and such a direct occupation of the mind with heavenly thoughts, that to enjoy the blessing would imply a withdrawing of oneself from all the ordinary avocations of life. This is the same error as drove the first monks into the wilderness.

—

81

Blessed be God, there is no necessity for such a going out of the world. Abiding in Jesus is not a work that needs each moment the mind to be engaged, or the affections to be directly and actively occupied with it. It is an entrusting of oneself to the keeping of the Eternal Love, in the faith that it will abide near us, and with its holy presence watch over us and ward off the evil, even when we have to be most intently occupied with other things. And so the heart has rest and peace and joy in the consciousness of being kept when it cannot keep itself.

In ordinary life, we have abundant illustration of the influence of a supreme affection reigning in and guarding the soul, while the mind concentrates itself on work that requires its whole attention. Think of the father of a family, separated for a time from his home, that he may secure for his loved ones what they need. He loves his wife and children, and longs much to return to them. There may be hours of intense occupation when he has not a moment to think of them, and yet his love is as deep and real as when he can call up their images; all the while his love and the hope of making them happy urge him on, and fill him with a secret joy in his work. Think of a king: in the midst of work, and pleasure, and trial, he all the while acts under the secret influence of the consciousness of royalty, even while he does not think of it. A loving wife and mother never for one moment loses the sense of her relation to the husband and children: the consciousness and the love are there, amid all her engagements. And shall it be thought impossible for the Everlasting Love so to take and keep possession of our spirits, that we too shall never for a moment lose the secret consciousness: We are in Christ, kept in Him by His almighty power. Oh, it is possible; we can be sure it is. Our abiding in Jesus is even more than a fellowship of love -- it is a fellowship of life. In work or in rest, the consciousness of life never leaves us. And even so can the mighty power of the Eternal Life maintain within us the consciousness of its presence. Or rather, Christ, who is our life, Himself dwells within us, and by His presence maintains our consciousness that we are in Him.

82

The second objection has reference to our sinfulness. Christians are so accustomed to look upon sinning daily as something absolutely inevitable, that they regard it as a matter of course that no one can keep up abiding fellowship with the Saviour: we must sometimes be unfaithful and fail. As if it was not just because we have a nature which is naught but a very fountain of sin, that the abiding in Christ has been ordained for us as our only but our sufficient deliverance! As if it were not the Heavenly Vine, the living, loving Christ, in whom we have to abide, and whose almighty power to hold us fast is to be the measure of our expectations! As if He would give us the command, "Abide in me," without securing the grace and the power to enable us to perform it! As if, above all, we had not the Father as the Husbandman to keep us from falling, and that not in a large and general sense, but according to His own precious promise: "Night and day, every moment!" Oh, if we will but look to our God as the Keeper of Israel, of whom it is said, "Jehovah shall keep thee from all evil; He shall keep thy soul," we shall learn to believe that conscious abiding in Christ every moment, night and day, is indeed what God has prepared for them that love Him.

—

My beloved fellow-Christians, let nothing less than this be your aim. I know well that you may not find it easy of attainment; that there may come more than one hour of weary struggle and bitter failure. Were the Church of Christ what it should be -- were older believers to younger converts what they should be, witnesses to God's faithfulness, like Caleb and Joshua, encouraging their brethren to go up and possess the land with their, "We are well able to overcome; if the Lord delight in us, then HE WILL BRING us into this land" -- were the atmosphere which the young believer breathes as he enters the fellowship of the saints that of a healthy, trustful, joyful consecration, abiding in Christ would come as the natural outgrowth of being in Him. But in the sickly state in which such a great part of the body is, souls that are pressing after this blessing are sorely hindered by the depressing influence of the thought and the life around them. It is not to discourage that I say this, but to warn, and to urge to a more entire casting of ourselves upon the word of God Himself. There may come more than our hour in which you are ready to yield to despair; but be of good courage. Only believe. He who has put the blessing within your reach will assuredly lead to its possession.

The way in which souls enter into the possession may differ. To some it may come as the gift of a moment. In times of revival, in the fellowship with other believers in whom the Spirit is working effectually, under the leading of some servant of God who can guide, and sometimes in solitude too, it is as if all at once a new revelation comes upon the soul. It sees, as in the light of heaven, the strong Vine holding and bearing the feeble branches so securely, that doubt becomes impossible. It can only wonder how it ever could have understood the words to mean aught else than this: To abide unceasingly in Christ is the portion of every believer. It sees it; and to believe, and rejoice, and love, come as of itself.

—

84

To others it comes by a slower and more difficult path. Day by day, amid discouragement and difficulty, the soul has to press forward. Be of good cheer; this way too leads to the rest. Seek but to keep your heart set upon the promise: "I THE LORD DO KEEP IT, night and day." Take from His own lips the watchword: "Every moment." In that you have the law of His love, and the law of your hope. Be content with nothing less. Think no longer that the duties and the cares, that the sorrows and the sins of this life must succeed in hindering the abiding life of fellowship. Take rather for the rule of your daily experience the language of faith: I am persuaded that neither death with its fears, nor life with its cares, nor things present with their pressing claims, nor things to come with their dark shadows, nor height of joy, nor depth of sorrow, nor any other creature, shall be able, for one single moment, to separate us from the love of God which is in Christ Jesus our Lord, and in which He is teaching me to abide. If things look dark and faith would fail, sing again the song of the vineyard: "I the Lord do keep it; I will water it every moment: lest any hurt it, I will keep it night and day." And be assured that, if Jehovah keep the branch night and day, and water it every moment, a life of continuous and unbroken fellowship with Christ is indeed our privilege.

Chapter 14 -- Day By Day

"And the people shall go out and gather the portion of a day in his day."-- Ex.16:4(marg.).

The day's portion in its day: Such was the rule for God's giving and man's working in the ingathering of the manna. It is still the law in all the dealings of God's grace with His children. A clear insight into the beauty and application of this arrangement is a wonderful help in understanding how one, who feels himself utterly weak, can have the confidence and the perseverance to hold on brightly through all the years of his earthly course. A doctor was once asked by a patient who had met with a serious accident: "Doctor, how long shall I have to lie here?" The answer, "Only a day at a time," taught the patient a precious lesson. It was the same lesson God had recorded for His people of all ages long before: The day's portion in its day.

It was, without doubt, with a view to this and to meet man's weakness, that God graciously appointed the change of day and night. If time had been given to man in the form of one long unbroken day, it would have exhausted and overwhelmed him; the change of day and night continually recruits and recreates his powers. As a child, who easily makes himself master of a book, when each day only the lesson for the day is given him, would be utterly hopeless if the whole book were given him at once; so it would be with man, if there were no divisions in time. Broken small and divided into fragments, he can bear them; only the care and the work of each day have to be undertaken -- the day's portion in its day. The rest of the night fits him for making a fresh start with each new morning; the mistakes of the past can be avoided, its lessons improved. And he has only each day to be faithful for the one short day, and long years and a long life take care of themselves, without the sense of their length or their weight ever being a burden.

Most sweet is the encouragement to be derived from this truth in the life of grace. Many a soul is disquieted with the thought as to how it will be able to gather and to keep the manna needed for all its years of travel through such a barren wilderness. It has never learnt what unspeakable comfort there is in the word: The day's portion for its day. That word takes away all care for the morrow most completely. Only to-day is yours; to-morrow is the Father's. The question: What security have you that during all the years in which you have to contend with the coldness, or temptations, or trials of the world, you will always abide in Jesus? is one you need, yea, you may not ask. Manna, as your food and strength, is given only by the day; faithfully to fill the present is your only security for the future. Accept, and enjoy, and fulfil with your whole heart the part you have this day to perform. His presence and grace enjoyed to-day will remove all doubt whether you can entrust the morrow to Him too.

How great the value which this truth teaches us to attach to each single day! We are so easily led to look at life as a great whole, and to neglect the little to-day, to forget that the single days do indeed make up the whole, and that the value of each single day depends on its influence on the whole. One day lost is a link broken in the chain, which it often takes more than another day to mend. One day lost influences the next,and makes its keeping more difficult. Yea, one day lost may be the loss of what months or years of careful labour had secured. The experience of many a believer could confirm this.

Believer! would you abide in Jesus, let it be day by day. You have already heard the message: Moment by moment; the lesson of day by day has something more to teach. Of the moments there are many where there is no direct exercise of the mind on your part; the abiding is in the deeper recesses of the heart, kept by the Father, to whom you entrusted yourself. But just this is the work that with each new day has to be renewed for the day -- the distinct renewal of surrender and trust for the life of moment by moment. God has gathered up the moments and bound them up into a bundle, for the very purpose that we might take measure of them. As we look forward in the morning, or look back in the evening, and weigh the moments, we learn how to value and how to use them rightly. And even as the Father, with each new morning, meets you with the promise of just sufficient manna for the day for yourself and those who have to partake with you, meet Him with the bright and loving renewal of your acceptance of the position He has given you in His beloved Son. Accustom yourself to look upon this as one of the reasons for the appointment of day and night. God thought of our weakness, and sought to provide for it. Let each day have its value from your calling to abide in Christ. As its light opens on your waking eyes, accept it on these terms: A day, just one day only, but still a day, given to abide and grow up in Jesus Christ. Whether it be a day of health or sickness, joy or sorrow, rest or work, of struggle or victory, let the chief thought with which you receive it in the morning thanksgiving be this: "A day that the Father gave; in it I may, I must become more closely united to Jesus." As the Father asks, "Can you trust me just for this one day to keep you abiding in Jesus, and Jesus to keep you fruitful?" you cannot but give the joyful response: "I will trust and not be afraid."

—

The day's portion for its day was given to Israel in the morning very early. The portion was for use and nourishment during the whole day, but the giving and the getting of it was the morning's work. This suggests how greatly the power to spend a day aright, to abide all the day in Jesus, depends on the morning hour. If the first-fruits be holy, the lump is holy. During the day there come hours of intense occupation in the rush of business or the throng of men, when only the Father's keeping can maintain the connection with Jesus unbroken. The morning manna fed all the day; it is only when the believer in the morning secures his quiet time in secret to renew distinctly and effectually loving fellowship with his Saviour, that the abiding can be kept up all the day. But what cause for thanksgiving that it may be done! In the morning, with its freshness and quiet, the believer can look out upon the day. He can consider its duties and its temptations, and pass them through beforehand, as it were, with his Saviour, throwing all upon Him who has undertaken to be everything to him. Christ is his manna, his nourishment, his strength, his life: he can take the day's portion for the day, Christ as his for all the needs the day may bring, and go on in the assurance that the day will be one of blessing and of growth.

And then, as the lesson of the value and the work of the single day is being taken to heart, the learner is all unconsciously being led on to get the secret of "day by day continually" (Ex.29:38). The blessed abiding grasped by faith for each day apart is an unceasing and ever-increasing growth. Each day of faithfulness brings a blessing for the next; makes both the trust and the surrender easier and more blessed. And so the Christian life grows: as we give our whole heart to the work of each day, it becomes all the day, and from that every day. And so each day separately, all the day continually, day by day successively, we abide in Jesus. And the days make up the life: what once appeared too high and too great to attain, is given to the soul that was content to take and use "every day his portion" (Ezra 3:4), "as the duty of every day required." Even here on earth the voice is heard: "Well done, good and faithful servant, thou hast been faithful over few, I will make thee ruler over many: enter thou into the joy of thy Lord." Our daily life becomes a wonderful interchange of God's daily grace and our daily praise: "Daily He loadeth us with His benefits"; "that I may daily perform my vows." We learn to understand God's reason for daily giving, as He most certainly gives, only enough, but also fully enough, for each day. And we get into His way, the way of daily asking and expecting only enough, but most certainly fully enough, for the day. We begin to number our days not from the sun's rising over the world, or by the work we do or the food we eat, but the daily renewal of the miracle of the manna -- the blessedness of daily fellowship with Him who is the Life and the Light of the world. The heavenly life is as unbroken and continuous as the earthly; the abiding in Christ each day has for that day brought its blessing; we abide in Him every day, and all the day. Lord, make this the portion of each one of us.

Chapter 15 -- At This Moment

"Behold, NOW is the accepted time; behold, NOW is the day of salvation." -- 2 Cor 6:2

The thought of living moment by moment is of such central importance -- looking at the abiding in Christ from our side -- that we want once more to speak of it. And to all who desire to learn the blessed art of living only a moment at a time, we want to say: The way to learn it is to exercise yourself in living in the present moment. Each time your attention is free to occupy itself with the thought of Jesus -- whether it be with time to think and pray, or only for a few passing seconds -- let your first thought be to say: Now, at this moment, I do abide in Jesus. Use such time, not in vain regrets that you have not been abiding fully, or still more hurtful fears that you will not be able to abide, but just at once take the position the Father has given you: "I am in Christ; this is the place God has given me. I accept it; here I rest; I do now abide in Jesus." This is the way to learn to abide continually. You may be yet so feeble as to fear to say of each day, "I am abiding in Jesus"; but the feeblest can, each single moment, say, as he consents to occupy his place as a branch in the vine, "Yes, I do abide in Christ." It is not a matter of feeling -- it is not a question of growth or strength in the Christian life -- it is the simple question whether the will at the present moment desires and consents to recognise the place you have in your Lord, and to accept it. If you are a believer, you are in Christ. If you are in Christ, and wish to stay there, it is your duty to say, though it be but for a moment, "Blessed Saviour, I abide in Thee now; Thou keepest me now."

It has been well said that in that little word now lies one of the deepest secrets of the life of faith. At the close of a conference on the spiritual life, a minister of experience rose and spoke. He did not know that he had learnt any truth he did not know before, but he had learnt how to use aright what he had known. He had learnt that it was his privilege at each moment, whatever surrounding circumstances might be, to say, "Jesus saves me now." This is indeed the secret of rest and victory. If I can say, "Jesus is to me at this moment all that God gave Him to be -- life, and strength, and peace" -- I have but as I say it to hold still, and rest, and realize it, and for that moment I have what I need. As my faith sees how of God I am in Christ, and takes the place in Him my Father has provided, my soul can peacefully settle down: Now I abide in Christ.

Believer! when striving to find the way to abide in Christ from moment to moment, remember that the gateway is: Abide in Him at this present moment. Instead of wasting effort in trying to get into a state that will last, just remember that it is Christ Himself, the living, loving Lord, who alone can keep you, and is waiting to do so. Begin at once and act faith in Him for the present moment: this is the only way to be kept the next. To attain the life of permanent and perfect abiding is not ordinarily given at once as a possession for the future: it comes mostly step by step. Avail yourself, therefore, of every opportunity of exercising the trust of the present moment. Each time you bow in prayer, let there first be an act of simple devotion: "Father, I am in Christ; I now abide in Him." Each time you have, amidst the bustle of duty, the opportunity of self-recollection, let its first involuntary act be: "I am still in Christ, abiding in Him now." Even when overtaken by sin, and the heart within is all disturbed and excited, O let your first look upwards be with the words: "Father, I have sinned; and yet I come -- though I blush to say it -- as one who is in Christ. Father! here I am; I can take no other place; of God I am in Christ; I now abide in Christ." Yes, Christian, in every possible circumstance, every moment of the day, the voice is calling: Abide in me, do it now. And even now, as you are reading this, O come at once and enter upon the blessed life of always abiding, by doing it at once: do it now.

94

In the life of David there is a beautiful passage which may help to make this thought clearer (2 Sam.3:17,18). David had been anointed king in Judah. The other tribes still followed Ish-bosheth, Saul's son. Abner, Saul's chief captain, resolves to lead the tribes of Israel to submit to David, the God-appointed king of the whole nation. He speaks to the elders of Israel: "Ye sought for David in times past to be king over you; now, then, do it, for Jehovah hath spoken of David, saying, By the hand of my servant David will I save my people Israel out of the hand of the Philistines, and out of the hand of all their enemies." And they did it, and anointed David a second time to be king, now over all Israel, as at first only over Judah (2 Sam.5:3) -- a most instructive type of the way in which a soul is led to the life of entire surrender and undivided allegiance, to the full abiding.

First you have the divided kingdom: Judah faithful to the king of God's appointment; Israel still clinging to the king of its own choosing. As a consequence, the nation divided against itself, and no power to conquer the enemies. Picture of the divided heart. Jesus accepted as King in Judah, the place of the holy mount, in the inner chamber of the soul; but the surrounding territory, the every-day life, not yet brought to subjection; more than half the life still ruled by self-will and its hosts. And so no real peace within and no power over the enemies.

Then there is the longing desire for a better state: "Ye sought for David in times past to be king over you." There was a time, when David had conquered the Philistines, that Israel believed in him; but they had been led astray. Abner appeals to their own knowledge of God's will, that David must rule over all. So the believer, when first brought to Jesus, did indeed want Him to be Lord over all, had hoped that He alone would be King. But, alas! unbelief and self-will had come in, and Jesus could not assert His power over the whole life. And yet the Christian is not content. How he longs -- sometimes without daring to hope that it can be -- for a better time.

Then follows God's promise. Abner says: "The Lord hath spoken, By the hand of David I will save my people from the hand of all their enemies." He appeals to God's promise: as David had conquered the Philistines, the nearest enemy in time past, so he alone could conquer those farther off. He should save Israel from the hand of all their enemies. Beautiful type of the promise by which the soul is now invited to trust Jesus for the victory over every enemy, and a life of undisturbed fellowship. "The Lord hath spoken" -- this is our only hope. On that word rests the sure expectation (Luke 1:70-75): "As He spake, That we should be saved from the hand of all that hate us, to perform the oath which He sware, that He would grant unto us that we, being delivered from the hand of our enemies, should serve Him without fear, in holiness and righteousness before Him, all the days of our life." David reigning over every corner of the land, and leading a united and obedient people on from victory to victory: this is the promise of what Jesus can do for us, as soon as in faith in God's promise all is surrendered to Him, and the whole life given up to be kept abiding in Him.

"Ye sought for David in times past to be king over you," spake Abner, and added, "Then do it now." Do it now is the message that this story brings to each one of us who longs to give Jesus unreserved supremacy. Whatever the present moment be, however unprepared the message finds you, however sad the divided and hopeless state of the life may be, still I come and urge Christ's claim to an immediate surrender -- this very moment. I know well that it will take time for the blessed Lord to assert His power, and order all within you according to His will -- to conquer the enemies and train all your powers for His service. This is not the work of a moment. But there are things which are the work of a moment -- of this moment.

The one is -- your surrender of all to Jesus; your surrender of yourself entirely to live only in Him. As time goes on, and exercise has made faith stronger and brighter, that surrender may become clearer and more intelligent. But for this no one may wait. The only way ever to attain to it is to begin at once. Do it now. Surrender yourself this very moment to abide wholly, only, always in Jesus. It is the work of a moment. And just so, Christ's renewed acceptance of you is the work of a moment. Be assured that He has you and holds you as His own, and that each new "Jesus, I do abide in Thee," meets with an immediate and most hearty response from the Unseen One. No act of faith can be in vain. He does indeed anew take hold on us and draw us close to Himself. Therefore, as often as the message comes, or the thought of it comes, Jesus says: Abide in me, do it at once. Each moment there is the whisper: Do it now.

Let any Christian begin, then, and he will speedily experience how the blessing of the present moment is passed on to the next. It is the unchanging Jesus to whom he links himself; it is the power of a divine life, in its unbroken continuity, that takes possession of him. The do it now of the present moment -- a little thing though it seems -- is nothing less than the beginning of the ever-present now, which is the mystery and the glory of eternity. Therefore, Christian, abide in Christ: do it now.

Chapter 16 -- Forsaking All For Him

"I have suffered the loss of all things, and do count them but dung, that I may win Christ, and be found IN HIM." -- Phil.3:8-9.

Wherever there is life, there is a continual interchange of taking in and giving out, receiving and restoring. The nourishment I take is given out again in the work I do; the impressions I receive, in the thoughts and feelings I express. The one depends on the other -- the giving out ever increases the power of taking in. In the healthy exercise of giving and taking is all the enjoyment of life.

It is so in the spiritual life too. There are Christians who look on its blessedness as consisting all in the privilege of ever receiving; they know not how the capacity for receiving is only kept up and enlarged by continual giving up and giving out -- how it is only in the emptiness that comes from the parting with what we have, that the divine fulness can flow in. It was a truth our Saviour continually insisted on. When He spoke of selling all to secure the treasure, of losing our life to find it, of the hundred-fold to those who forsake all, He was expounding the need of self-sacrifice as the law of the Kingdom for Himself as well as for His disciples. If we are really to abide in Christ, and to be found in Him -- to have our life always and wholly in Him -- we must each in our measure say with Paul, "I count all things but loss for the excellency of the knowledge of Christ Jesus my Lord, that I may win Christ, and be FOUND IN Him."

Let us try and see what there is to be forsaken and given up. First of all, there is sin. There can be no true conversion without the giving up of sin. And yet, owing to the ignorance of the young convert of what really is sin, of what the claims of God's holiness are, and what the extent to which the power of Jesus can enable us to conquer sin, the giving up of sin is but partial and superficial. With the growth of the Christian life there comes the want of a deeper and more entire purging out of everything that is unholy. And it is specially when the desire to abide in Christ uninterruptedly, to be always found in Him, becomes strong, that the soul is led to see the need of a new act of surrender, in which it afresh accepts and ratifies its death to sin in Christ, and parts indeed with everything that is sin. Availing himself, in the strength of God's Spirit, of that wonderful power of our nature by which the whole of one's future life can be gathered up and disposed of in one act of the will, the believer yields himself to sin no more -- to be only and wholly a servant of righteousness. He does it in the joyful assurance that every sin surrendered is gain indeed -- room for the inflowing of the presence and the love of Christ.

Next to the parting with unrighteousness, is the giving up of self-righteousness. Though contending most earnestly against our own works or merits, it is often long before we come really to understand what it is to refuse self the least place or right in the service of God. Unconsciously we allow the actings of our own mind and heart and will free scope in God's presence. In prayer and worship, in Bible reading and working for God, instead of absolute dependence on the Holy Spirit's leading, self is expected to do a work it never can do. We are slow to learn the lesson, "In me, that is, in my flesh, dwelleth no good thing." As it is learnt, and we see how corruption extends to everything that is of nature, we see that there can be no entire abiding in Christ without the giving up of all that is of self in religion -- without giving it up to the death, and waiting for the breathings of the Holy Spirit as alone able to work in us what is acceptable in God's sight.

Then, again, there is our whole natural life, with all the powers and endowments bestowed upon us by the Creator, with all the occupations and interests with which Providence has surrounded us. It is not enough that, when once you are truly converted, you have the earnest desire to have all these devoted to the service of the Lord. The desire is good, but can neither teach the way nor give the strength to do it acceptably. Incalculable harm has been done to the deeper spirituality of the Church, by the idea that when once we are God's children the using of our gifts in His service follows as a matter of course. No; for this there is indeed needed very special grace. And the way in which the grace comes is again that of sacrifice and surrender. I must see how all my gifts and powers are, even though I be a child of God, still defiled by sin, and under the power of the flesh. I must feel that I cannot at once proceed to use them for God's glory. I must first lay them at Christ's feet, to be accepted and cleansed by Him. I must feel myself utterly powerless to use them aright. I must see that they are most dangerous to me, because through them the flesh, the old nature, self, will so easily exert its power. In this conviction I must part with them, giving them entirely up to the Lord. When He has accepted them, and set His stamp upon them, I receive them back, to hold them as His property, to wait on Him for the grace to use them aright day by day, and to have them act only under His influence. And so experience proves it true here too, that the path of entire consecration is the path of full salvation. Not only is what is thus given up received back again to become doubly our own, but the forsaking all is followed by the receiving all. We abide in Christ more fully as we forsake all and follow Him. As I count all things loss for His sake, I am found IN Him.

The same principle holds good of all the lawful occupations and possessions with which we are entrusted of God. Such were the fish-nets on the Sea of Galilee, and the household duties of Martha of Bethany -- the home and the friends of many a one among Jesus' disciples. Jesus taught them in very deed to forsake all for Him. It was no arbitrary command, but the simple application of a law in nature to the Kingdom of His grace -- that the more perfectly the old occupant is cast out, the more complete can be the possession of the new, and the more entire the renewal of all within.

This principle has a still deeper application. The truly spiritual gifts which are the working of God's own Holy Spirit within us -- these surely need not be thus given up and surrendered? They do indeed; the interchange of giving up and taking in is a life process, and may not cease for a moment. No sooner does the believer begin to rejoice in the possession of what he has, than the inflow of new grace is retarded, and stagnation threatens. It is only into the thirst of an empty soul that the streams of living waters flow. Ever thirsting is the secret of never thirsting. Each blessed experience we receive as a gift of God, must at once be returned back to Him from whom it came, in praise and love, in self-sacrifice and service; so only can it be restored to us again, fresh and beautiful with the bloom of heaven. Is not this the wonderful lesson Isaac on Moriah teaches us? Was he not the son of promise, the God-given life, the wonder-gift of the omnipotence of Him who quickeneth the dead? (Rom.4:17). And yet even he had to be given up, and sacrificed, that he might be received back again a thousandfold more precious than before -- a type of the Only-begotten of the Father, whose pure and holy life had to be given up ere He could receive it again in resurrection power, and could make His people partakers of it. A type, too, of what takes place in the life of each believer, as, instead of resting content with past experiences or present grace, he presses on, forgetting and giving up all that is behind, and reaches out to the fullest possible apprehension of Christ His life.

And such surrender of all for Christ, is it a single step, the act and experience of a moment, or is it a course of daily renewed and progressive attainment? It is both. There may be a moment in the life of a believer when he gets a first sight, or a deeper insight, of this most blessed truth, and when, made willing in the day of God's power, he does indeed, in an act of the will, gather up the whole of life yet before him into the decision of a moment, and lay himself on the altar a living and an acceptable sacrifice. Such moments have often been the blessed transition from a life of wandering and failure to a life of abiding and power divine. But even then his daily life becomes, what the life must be of each one who has no such experience, the unceasing prayer for more light on the meaning of entire surrender, the ever-renewed offering up of all he has to God.

Believer, would you abide in Christ, see here the blessed path. Nature shrinks back from such self-denial and crucifixion in its rigid application to our life in its whole extent. But what nature does not love and cannot perform, grace will accomplish, and make to you a life of joy and glory. Do you but yield up yourself to Christ your Lord; the conquering power of His incoming presence will make it joy to cast out all that before was most precious. "A hundredfold in this life": this word of the Master comes true to all who, with whole-hearted faithfulness, accept His commands to forsake all. The blessed receiving soon makes the giving up most blessed too. And the secret of a life of close abiding will be seen to be simply this: As I give myself wholly to Christ, I find the power to take Him wholly for myself; and as I lose myself and all I have for Him, He takes me wholly for Himself, and gives Himself wholly to me.

Chapter 17 -- Through The Holy Spirit

"The anointing which ye have received of him, abideth in you; and even as it hath taught you, ye shall abide in him." – 1 John 2:27.

How beautiful the thought of a life always abiding in Christ! The longer we think of it, the more attractive it becomes. And yet how often it is that the precious words, "Abide in me," are heard by the young disciple with a sigh! It is as if he understands so little what they really mean, and can realize so little how this full enjoyment can be attained. He longs for some one who could make it perfectly clear, and continually again remind him that the abiding is in very deed within his reach. If such an one would but listen to the word we have from John this day, what hope and joy it would bring! It gives us the divine assurance that we have the anointing of the Holy Spirit to teach us all things, also to teach us how to abide in Christ.

Alas! someone answers, this word does not give me comfort, it only depresses me more. For it tells of another privilege I so little know to enjoy: I do not understand how the teaching of the Spirit is given -- where or how I can discern His voice. If the Teacher is so unknown, no wonder that the promise of His teaching about the abiding does not help me much.

Thoughts like these come from an error which is very common among believers. They imagine that the Spirit, in teaching them, must reveal the mysteries of the spiritual life first to their intellect, and afterwards in their experience. And God's way is just the contrary of this. What holds true of all spiritual truth is specially true of the abiding in Christ: We must live and experience truth in order to know it. Life-fellowship with Jesus is the only school for the science of heavenly things. "What I do, thou knowest not now, but thou shalt know hereafter," is a law of the Kingdom, specially true of the daily cleansing of which it first was spoken, and the daily keeping. Receive what you do not comprehend, submit to what you cannot understand, accept and expect what to reason appears a mystery, believe what looks impossible, walk in a way which you know not -- such are the first lessons in the school of God. "If ye abide in my word, ye shall understand the truth": in these and other words of God we are taught that there is a habit of mind and life which precedes the understanding of the truth. True discipleship consists in first following, and then knowing the Lord. The believing surrender to Christ, and the submission to His word to expect what appears most improbable, is the only way to the full blessedness of knowing Him.

These principles hold specially good in regard to the teaching of the Spirit. That teaching consists in His guiding the spiritual life within us to that which God has prepared for us, without our always knowing how. On the strength of God's promise, and trusting in His faithfulness, the believer yields himself to the leading of the Holy Spirit, without claiming to have it first made clear to the intellect what He is to do, but consenting to let Him do His work in the soul, and afterwards to know what He has wrought there. Faith trusts the working of the Spirit unseen in the deep recesses of the inner life. And so the word of Christ and the gift of the Spirit are to the believer sufficient guarantee that He will be taught of the Spirit to abide in Christ. By faith he rejoices in what he does not see or feel: he knows, and is confident that the blessed Spirit within is doing His work silently but surely, guiding him into the life of full abiding and unbroken communion. The Holy Spirit is the Spirit of life in Christ Jesus; it is His work, not only to breathe, but ever to foster and strengthen, and so to perfect the new life within. And just in proportion as the believer yields himself in simple trust to the unseen, but most certain law of the Spirit of life working within him, his faith will pass into knowledge. It will be rewarded by the Spirit's light revealing in the Word what has already been wrought by the Spirit's power in the life.

Apply this now to the promise of the Spirit's teaching us to abide in Christ. The Holy Spirit is indeed the mighty power of God. And He comes to us from the heart of Christ, the bearer of Christ's life, the revealer and communicator of Christ Himself within us. In the expression, "the fellowship of the Spirit," we are taught what His highest work is. He is the bond of fellowship between the Father and the Son: by Him they are one. He is the bond of fellowship between all believers: by Him they are one. Above all, He is the bond of fellowship between Christ and believers ; He is the life-sap through which Vine and branch grow into real and living oneness: by Him we are one. And we can be assured of it, that if we do but believe in His presence and working, if we do but watch not to grieve Him, because we know that He is in us, if we wait and pray to be filled with Him, He will teach us how to abide. First guiding our will to a whole-hearted cleaving to Christ, then quickening our faith into ever larger confidence and expectation, then breathing into our hearts a peace and joy that pass understanding, He teaches us to abide, we scarce know how. Then coming through the heart and life into the understanding, He makes us know the truth -- not as mere thought-truth, but as the truth which is in Christ Jesus, the reflection into the mind of the light of what He has already made a reality in the life. "The life was the light of men."

In view of such teaching, it is clear how, if we would have the Spirit to guide us into the abiding life, our first need is -- quiet restful faith. Amid all the questions and difficulties that may come up in connection with our striving to abide in Christ -- amid all the longing we may sometimes feel to have a Christian of experience to aid us -- amid the frequent painful consciousness of failure, of ignorance, of helplessness -- do let us hold fast the blessed confidence: We have the unction of the Holy One to teach us to abide in Him.

"THE ANOINTING which ye have received of Him, ABIDETH IN you; and even as it hath taught you, YE SHALL ABIDE IN Him." Make this teaching of His in connection with the abiding a matter of special exercise of faith. Believe that as surely as you have part in Christ, you have His Spirit too. Believe that He will do His work with power, if only you do not hinder Him. Believe that He is working,even when you cannot discern it. Believe that He will work mightily if you ask this from the Father. It is impossible to live the life of full abiding without being full of the the Holy Spirit; believe that the fulness of the Spirit is indeed your daily portion. Be sure and take time in prayer to dwell at the footstool of the throne of God and the Lamb, whence flows the river of the water of life. It is there, and only there, that you can be filled with the Spirit. Cultivate carefully the habit of daily, yea, continually honouring Him by the quiet, restful confidence that He is doing His work within. Let faith in His indwelling make you jealous of whatever could grieve Him -- the spirit of the world or the actings of self and the flesh. Let that faith seek its nourishment in the Word and all it says of the Spirit, His power, His comfort, and His work. Above all, let that faith in the Spirit's indwelling lead you specially, to look away to Jesus; as we have received the anointing of Him, it comes in ever stronger flow from Him as we are occupied with Him alone. Christ is the Anointed One. As we look up to Him, the holy anointing comes, "the precious ointment upon the head of Aaron, that went down to the skirts of his garments." It is faith in Jesus that brings the anointing; the anointing leads to Jesus, and to the abiding in Him alone.

Believer, abide in Christ, in the power of the Spirit. What think you, ought the abiding longer to be a fear or a burden? Surely not. Oh, if we did but know the graciousness of our Holy Comforter, and the blessedness of wholly yielding ourselves to His leading, we should indeed experience the divine comfort of having such a teacher to secure our biding in Christ. The Holy Spirit was given for this one purpose -- that the glorious redemption and life in Christ might with divine power be conveyed and communicated to us. We have the Holy Spirit to make the living Christ, in all His saving power, and in the completeness of His victory over sin, ever present within us. It is this that constitutes Him the Comforter: with Him we need never mourn an absent Christ. Let us therefore, as often as we read, or meditate, or pray in connection with this abiding in Christ, reckon upon it as a settled thing that we have the Spirit of God Himself within us, teaching, and guiding, and working. Let us rejoice in the confidence that we must succeed in our desires, because the Holy Spirit is working all the while with secret but divine power in the soul that does not hinder Him by its unbelief.

Chapter 18 -- In Stillness Of Soul

"In returning and rest shall ye be saved; in quietness and confidence shall be your strength." -- Isa 30:15
"Be silent to the Lord, and wait patiently for him." -- Ps.37:7 (marg.)
"Truly my soul is silent unto God." -- Ps.62:1 (marg.)

There is a view of the Christian life that regards it as a sort of partnership, in which God and man have each to do their part. It admits that it is but little that man can do, and that little defiled with sin; still he must do his utmost -- then only can he expect God to do His part. To those who think thus,it is extremely difficult to understand what Scripture means when it speaks of our being still and doing nothing, of our resting and waiting to see the salvation of God. It appears to them a perfect contradiction, when we speak of this quietness and ceasing from all effort as the secret of the highest activity of man and all his powers. And yet this is just what Scripture does teach. The explanation of the apparent mystery is to be found in this, that when God and man are spoken of as working together, there is nothing of the idea of a partnership between two partners who each contribute their share to a work. The relation is a very different one. The true idea is that of cooperation founded on subordination. As Jesus was entirely dependent on the Father for all His words and all His works, so the believer can do nothing of himself. What he can do of himself is altogether sinful. He must therefore cease entirely from his own doing, and wait for the working of God in him. As he ceases from self-effort, faith assures him that God does what He has undertaken, and works in him. And what God does is to renew, to sanctify, and waken all his energies to their highest power. So that just in proportion as he yields himself a truly passive instrument in the hand of God, will he be wielded of God as the active instrument of His almighty power. The soul in which the wondrous combination of perfect passivity with the highest activity is most completely realized, has the deepest experience of what the Christian life is.

Among the lessons to be learnt of those who are studying the blessed art of abiding in Christ, there is none more needful and more profitable than this one of stillness of soul. In it alone can we cultivate that teachableness of spirit, to which the Lord will reveal His secrets -- that meekness to which He shows His ways. It is the spirit exhibited so beautifully in all the three Marys: In her whose only answer to the most wonderful revelation ever made to human being was, "Behold the handmaid of the Lord; be it unto me according to Thy word"; and of whom, as mysteries multiplied around her, it is written: "Mary kept all these things and pondered them in her heart." And in her who "sat at Jesus' feet, and heard His word," and who showed, in the anointing Him for His burial, how she had entered more deeply into the mystery of His death than even the beloved disciple. And in her, too, who sought her Lord in the house of the Pharisee, with tears that spake more than words. It is a soul silent unto God that is the best preparation for knowing Jesus, and for holding fast the blessings He bestows. It is when the soul is hushed in silent awe and worship before the Holy Presence that reveals itself within, that the still small voice of the blessed Spirit will be heard.

Therefore, beloved Christian, as often as you seek to understand better the blessed mystery of abiding in Christ, let this be your first thought (Ps.62:5, marg.): "My soul, only be silent unto God; for my expectation is from Him." Do you in very deed hope to realize the wondrous union with the Heavenly Vine? Know that flesh and blood cannot reveal it unto you, but only the Father in heaven. "Cease from thine own wisdom." You have but to bow in the confession of your own ignorance and impotence; the Father will delight to give you the teaching of the Holy Spirit. If but your ear be open, and your thoughts brought into subjection, and your heart prepared in silence to wait upon God, and to hear what He speaks, He will reveal to you His secrets. And one of the first secrets will be the deeper insight into the truth, that as you sink low before Him in nothingness and helplessness, in a silence and a stillness of soul that seeks to catch the faintest whisper of His love, teachings will come to you which you had never heard before for the rush and noise of your own thoughts and efforts. You shall learn how your great work is to listen, and hear, and believe what He promises; to watch and wait and see what He does; and then, in faith, and worship, and obedience, to yield yourself to His working who works in you mightily.

One would think that no message could be more beautiful or welcome than this, that we may rest and be quiet, and that our God will work for us and in us. And yet how far this is from being the case! And how slow many are to learn that quietness is blessedness, that quietness is strength, that quietness is the source of the highest activity -- the secret of all true abiding in Christ! Let us try to learn it, and to watch against whatever interferes with it. The dangers that threaten the soul's rest are not a few.

There is the dissipation of soul which comes from entering needlessly and too deeply into the interests of this world. Every one of us has his divine calling; and within the circle pointed out by God Himself, interest in our work and its surroundings is a duty. But even here the Christian needs to exercise watchfulness and sobriety. And still more do we need a holy temperance in regard to things not absolutely imposed upon us by God. If abiding in Christ really be our first aim, let us beware of all needless excitement. Let us watch even in lawful and necessary things against the wondrous power these have to keep the soul so occupied, that there remains but little power or zest for fellowship with God. Then there is the restlessness and worry that come of care and anxiety about earthly things; these eat away the life of trust, and keep the soul like a troubled sea. There the gentle whispers of the Holy Comforter cannot be heard.

No less hurtful is the spirit of fear and distrust in spiritual things; with its apprehensions and its efforts, it never comes really to hear what God has to say. Above all, there is the unrest that comes of seeking in our own way and in our own strength the spiritual blessing which comes alone from above. The heart occupied with its own plans and efforts for doing God's will, and securing the blessing of abiding in Jesus, must fail continually. God's work is hindered by our interference. He can do His work perfectly only when the soul ceases from its work. He will do His work mightily in the soul that honours Him by expecting Him to work both to will and to do.

And, last of all, even when the soul seeks truly to enter the way of faith, there is the impatience of the flesh, which forms its judgment of the life and progress of the soul not after the divine but the human standard.

In dealing with all this, and so much more, blessed the man who learns the lesson of stillness, and fully accepts God's word: "In quietness and confidence shall be your strength." Each time he listens to the word of the Father, or asks the Father to listen to his words, he dares not begin his Bible reading or prayer without first pausing and waiting, until the soul be hushed in the presence of the Eternal Majesty. Under a sense of the divine nearness, the soul, feeling how self is always ready to assert itself, and intrude even into the holiest of all with its thoughts and efforts, yields itself in a quiet act of self-surrender to the teaching and working of the divine Spirit. It is still and waits in holy silence, until all is calm and ready to receive the revelation of the divine will and presence. Its reading and prayer then indeed become a waiting on God with ear and heart opened and purged to receive fully only what He says.

"Abide in Christ!" Let no one think that he can do this if he has not daily his quiet time, his seasons of meditation and waiting on God. In these a habit of soul must be cultivated, in which the believer goes out into the world and its distractions, the peace of God, that passeth all understanding, keeping the heart and mind. It is in such a calm and restful soul that the life of faith can strike deep root, that the Holy Spirit can give His blessed teaching, that the Holy Father can accomplish His glorious work. May each one of us learn every day to say, "Truly my soul is silent unto God." And may every feeling of the difficulty of attaining this only lead us simply to look and trust to Him whose presence makes even the storm a calm. Cultivate the quietness as a means to the abiding in Christ; expect the ever deepening quietness and calm of heaven in the soul as the fruit of abiding in Him.

Chapter 19 -- In Affliction And Trial

"Every branch that bearest fruit, he purgeth it, that it may bring forth more fruit." -- John 15:2.

In the whole plant world there is not a tree to be found so specially suited to the image of man in his relation to God, as the vine. There is none of which the fruit and its juice are so full of spirit, so quickening and stimulating. But there is also none of which the natural tendency is so entirely evil -- none where the growth is so ready to run into wood that is utterly worthless except for the fire. Of all plants, not one needs the pruning knife so unsparingly and so unceasingly. None is so dependent on cultivation and training, but with this none yields a richer reward to the husbandman. In His wonderful parable, the Saviour, with a single word, refers to this need of pruning in the vine, and the blessing it brings. But from that single word what streams of light pour in upon this dark world, so full of suffering and of sorrow to believers! What treasures of teaching and comfort to the bleeding branch in its hour of trial: "Every branch that beareth fruit, He purgeth it, that it may bring forth more fruit." And so He has prepared His people, who are so ready when trial comes to be shaken in their confidence, and to be moved from their abiding in Christ, to hear in each affliction the voice of a messenger that comes to call them to abide still more closely. Yes, believer, most specially in times of trial,abide in Christ.

Abide in Christ! This is indeed the Father's object in sending the trial. In the storm the tree strikes deeper roots in the soil; in the hurricane the inhabitants of the house abide within, and rejoice in its shelter. So by suffering the Father would lead us to enter more deeply into the love of Christ. Our hearts are continually prone to wander from Him; prosperity and enjoyment all too easily satisfy us, dull our spiritual perception, and unfit us for full communion with Himself. It is an unspeakable mercy that the Father comes with His chastisement, makes the world round us all dark and unattractive, leads us to feel more deeply our sinfulness, and for a time lose our joy in what was becoming so dangerous. He does it in the hope that, when we have found our rest in Christ in time of trouble, we shall learn to choose abiding in Him as our only portion; and when the affliction is removed, have so grown more firmly into Him, that in prosperity He still shall be our only joy. So much has He set His heart on this, that though He has indeed no pleasure in afflicting us, He will not keep back even the most painful chastisement if He can but thereby guide His beloved child to come home and abide in the beloved Son. Christian! pray for grace to see in every trouble, small or great, the Father's finger pointing to Jesus, and saying, Abide in Him.

Abide in Christ: so will you become partaker of all the rich blessings God designed for you in the affliction. The purposes of God's wisdom will become clear to you, your assurance of the unchangeable love become stronger, and the power of His Spirit fulfil you the promise: "He chasteneth us for our profit, that we might be partakers of His holiness." Abide in Christ: and your cross becomes the means of fellowship with His cross, and access into its mysteries -- the mystery of the curse which He bore for you, of the death to sin in which you partake with Him, of the love in which, as sympathizing High Priest, He descended into all your sorrows. Abide in Christ: growing in conformity to your blessed Lord in His sufferings, deeper experience of the reality and the tenderness of His love will be yours. Abide in Christ: in the fiery oven, one like the Son of Man will be seen as never before; the purging away of the dross and the refining of the gold will be accomplished, and Christ's own likeness reflected in you. O abide in Christ: the power of the flesh will be mortified, the impatience and self-will of the old nature be humbled, to make place for the meekness and gentleness of Christ. A believer may pass through much affliction, and yet secure but little blessing from it all. Abiding in Christ is the secret of securing all that the Father meant the chastisement to bring us.

Abide in Christ: in Him you shall find sure and abundant consolation. With the afflicted comfort is often first, and the profit of the affliction second. The Father loves us so, that with Him our real and abiding profit is His first object, but He does not forget to comfort too. When He comforts it is that He may turn the bleeding heart to Himself to receive the blessing in fellowship with Him; when He refuses comfort, His object is still the same. It is in making us partakers of His holiness that true comfort comes. The Holy Spirit is the Comforter, not only because He can suggest comforting thoughts of God's love, but far more, because He makes us holy, and brings us into close union with Christ and with God. He teaches us to abide in Christ; and because God is found there, the truest comfort will come there too. In Christ the heart of the Father is revealed, and higher comfort there cannot be than to rest in the Father's bosom. In Him the fulness of the divine love is revealed, combined with the tenderness of a mother's compassion -- and what can comfort like this? In Him you see a thousand times more given you than you have lost; see how God only took from you that you might have room to take from Him what is so much better. In Him suffering is consecrated, and becomes the foretaste of eternal glory; in suffering it is that the Spirit of God and of glory rests on us. Believer! would you have comfort in affliction? -- Abide in Christ.

Abide in Christ: so will you bear much fruit. Not a vine is planted but the owner thinks of the fruit, and the fruit only. Other trees may be planted for ornament, for the shade, for the wood -- the vine only for the fruit. And of each vine the husbandman is continually asking how it can bring forth more fruit, much fruit. Believer! abide in Christ in times of affliction, and you shall bring forth more fruit. The deeper experience of Christ's tenderness and the Father's love will urge you to live to His glory. The surrender of self and selfwill in suffering will prepare you to sympathize with the misery of others, while the softening that comes of chastisement will fit you for becoming, as Jesus was, the servant of all. The thought of the Father's desire for fruit in the pruning will lead you to yield yourself afresh, and more than ever, to Him, and to say that now you have but one object in life -- making known and conveying His wonderful love to fellow-men. You shall learn the blessed art of forgetting self, and, even in affliction, availing yourself of your separation from ordinary life to plead for the welfare of others. Dear Christian, in affliction abide in Christ. When you see it coming, meet it in Christ; when it is come, feel that you are more in Christ than in it, for He is nearer you than affliction ever can be; when it is passing, still abide in Him. And let the one thought of the Saviour, as He speaks of the pruning, and the one desire of the Father, as He does the pruning, be yours too: "Every branch that beareth fruit, He purgeth, that it may bring forth more fruit."

So shall your times of affliction become your times of choicest blessing -- preparation for richest fruitfulness. Led into closer fellowship with the Son of God, and deeper experience of His love and grace -- established in the blessed confidence that He and you entirely belong to each other -- more completely satisfied with Him and more wholly given up to Him than ever before -- with your own will crucified afresh, and the heart brought into deeper harmony with God's will -- you shall be a vessel cleansed, meet for the Master's use, prepared for every good work. True believer! O try and learn the blessed truth, that in affliction your first, your only, your blessed calling is to abide in Christ. Be much with Him alone. Beware of the comfort and the distractions that friends so often bring. Let Jesus Christ Himself be your chief companion and comforter. Delight yourself in the assurance that closer union with Him, and more abundant fruit through Him, are sure to be the results of trial, because it is the Husbandman Himself who is pruning, and will ensure the fulfilment of the desire of the soul that yields itself lovingly to His work.

Chapter 20 -- That You May Bear Much Fruit

"He that abideth in me, and I in him, the same bringeth forth much fruit. Herein is my Father glorified, that ye bear much fruit." -- John 15:5,8.

We all know what fruit is. The produce of the branch, by which men are refreshed and nourished. The fruit is not for the branch, but for those who come to carry it away. As soon as the fruit is ripe, the branch gives it off, to commence afresh its work of beneficence, and anew prepare its fruit for another season. A fruit-bearing tree lives not for itself, but wholly for those to whom its fruit brings refreshment and life. And so the branch exists only and entirely for the sake of the fruit. To make glad the heart of the husbandman is its object, its safety, and its glory.

Beautiful image of the believer, abiding in Christ! He not only grows in strength, the union with the Vine becoming ever surer and firmer, he also bears fruit, yea, much fruit. He has the power to offer that to others of which they can eat and live. Amid all who surround him he becomes like a tree of life, of which they can taste and be refreshed. He is in his circle a centre of life and of blessing, and that simply because he abides in Christ, and receives from Him the Spirit and the life of which he can impart to others. Learn thus, if you would bless others, to abide in Christ, and that if you do abide, you shall surely bless. As surely as the branch abiding in a fruitful vine bears fruit, so surely, yea, much more surely, will a soul abiding in Christ with His fulness of blessing be made a blessing.

The reason of this is easily understood. If Christ, the heavenly Vine, has taken the believer as a branch, then He has pledged Himself, in the very nature of things, to supply the sap and spirit and nourishment to make it bring forth fruit. "From ME is thy fruit found": these words derive new meaning from our parable. The soul need but have one care -- to abide closely, fully, wholly. He will give the fruit. He works all that is needed to make the believer a blessing.

Abiding in Him, you receive of Him His Spirit of love and compassion towards sinners, making you desirous to seek their good. By nature the heart is full of selfishness. Even in the believer, his own salvation and happiness are often too much his only object. But abiding in Jesus, you come into contact with His infinite love; its fire begins to burn within your heart; you see the beauty of love; you learn to look upon loving and serving and saving your fellow-men as the highest privilege a disciple of Jesus can have. Abiding in Christ, your heart learns to feel the wretchedness of the sinner still in darkness, and the fearfulness of the dishonour done to your God. With Christ you begin to bear the burden of souls, the burden of sins not your own. As you are more closely united to Him, somewhat of that passion for souls which urged Him to Calvary begins to breathe within you, and you are ready to follow His footsteps, to forsake the heaven of your own happiness, and devote your life to win the souls Christ has taught you to love. The very spirit of the Vine is love; the spirit of love streams into the branch that abides in Him.

The desire to be a blessing is but the beginning. As you undertake to work, you speedily become conscious of your own weakness and the difficulties in your way. Souls are not saved at your bidding. You are ready to be discouraged, and to relax your effort. But abiding in Christ, you receive new courage and strength for the work. Believing what Christ teaches, that it is HE who through you will give His blessing to the world, you understand that you are but the feeble instrument through which the hidden power of Christ does its work, that His strength may be perfected and made glorious in your weakness. It is a great step when the believer fully consents to his own weakness, and the abiding consciousness of it, and so works faithfully on, fully assured that his Lord is working through him. He rejoices that the excellence of the power is of God, and not of us. Realizing his oneness with his Lord, he considers no longer his own weakness, but counts on the power of Him of whose hidden working within he is assured. It is this secret assurance that gives a brightness to his look, and a gentle firmness to his tone, and a perseverance to all his efforts, which of themselves are great means of influencing those he is seeking to win. He goes forth in the spirit of one to whom victory is assured; for this is the victory that overcometh, even our faith. He no longer counts it humility to say that God cannot bless his unworthy efforts. He claims and expects a blessing, because it is not he, but Christ in him, that worketh. The great secret of abiding in Christ is the deep conviction that we are nothing, and He is everything. As this is learnt, it no longer seems strange to believe that our weakness need be no hindrance to His saving power. The believer who yields himself wholly up to Christ for service in the spirit of a simple, childlike trust, will assuredly bring forth much fruit. He will not fear even to claim his share in the wonderful promise: "He that believeth on me, the works that I do shall he do also; and greater works than these shall he do, because I go to the Father." He no longer thinks that He cannot have a blessing, and must be kept unfruitful, that he may be kept humble. He sees that the most heavily laden branches bow the lowest down. Abiding in Christ, he has yielded assent to the blessed agreement between the Vine and the branches, that of the fruit all the glory shall be to the Husbandman, the blessed Father.

Let us learn two lessons. If we are abiding in Jesus, let us begin to work. Let us first seek to influence those around us in daily life. Let us accept distinctly and joyfully our holy calling, that we are even now to live as the servants of the love of Jesus to our fellow-men. Our daily life must have for its object the making of an impression favourable to Jesus. When you look at the branch, you see at once the likeness to the Vine. We must live so that somewhat of the holiness and the gentleness of Jesus may shine out in us. We must live to represent Him. As was the case with Him when on earth, the life must prepare the way for the teaching. What the Church and the world both need is this: men and women full of the Holy Ghost and of love, who, as the living embodiments of the grace and power of Christ, witness for Him, and for His power on behalf of those who believe in Him. Living so, with our hearts longing to have Jesus glorified in the souls He is seeking after, let us offer ourselves to Him for direct work. There is work in our own home. There is work among the sick, the poor, and the outcast. There is work in a hundred different paths which the Spirit of Christ opens up through those who allow themselves to be led by Him. There is work perhaps for us in ways that have not yet been opened up by others. Abiding in Christ, let us work. Let us work, not like those who are content if they now follow the fashion, and take some share in religious work. No; let us work as those who are growing more like Christ, because they are abiding in Him, and who, like Him, count the work of winning souls to the Father the very joy and glory of heaven begun on earth.

And the second lesson is: If you work, abide in Christ. This is one of the blessings of work if done in the right spirit -- it will deepen your union with your blessed Lord. It will discover your weakness, and throw you back on His strength. It will stir you to much prayer; and in prayer for others is the time when the soul, forgetful of itself, unconsciously grows deeper into Christ. It will make clearer to you the true nature of branch-life; its absolute dependence, and at the same time its glorious sufficiency -- independent of all else, because dependent on Jesus. If you work, abide in Christ. There are temptations and dangers. Work for Christ has sometimes drawn away from Christ, and taken the place of fellowship with Him. Work can sometimes give a form of godliness without the power. As you work, abide in Christ. Let a living faith in Christ working in you be the secret spring of all your work; this will inspire at once humility and courage. Let the Holy Spirit of Jesus dwell in you as the Spirit of His tender compassion and His divine power. Abide in Christ, and offer every faculty of your nature freely and unreservedly to Him, to sanctify it for Himself. If Jesus Christ is really to work through us, it needs an entire consecration of ourselves to Him, daily renewed. But we understand now, just this is abiding in Christ; just this it is that constitutes our highest privilege and happiness. To be a branch bearing much fruit -- nothing less, nothing more -- be this our only joy.

Chapter 21 -- So Will You Have Power In Prayer

"If ye abide in me, and my words abide in you, ye shall ask what ye will, and it shall be done unto you. " -- John 15:7.

Prayer is both one of the means and one of the fruits of union to Christ. As a means it is of unspeakable importance. All the things of faith, all the pleadings of desire, all the yearnings after a fuller surrender, all the confessions of shortcoming and of sin, all the exercises in which the soul gives up self and clings to Christ, find their utterance in prayer. In each meditation on abiding in Christ, as some new feature of what Scripture teaches concerning this blessed life is apprehended, the first impulse of the believer is at once to look up to the Father and pour out the heart into His, and ask from Him the full understanding and the full possession of what he has been shown in the Word. And it is the believer, who is not content with this spontaneous expression of his hope, but who takes time in secret prayer to wait until he has received and laid hold of what he has seen, who will really grow strong in Christ. However feeble the soul's first abiding, its prayer will be heard, and it will find prayer one of the great means of abiding more abundantly.

But it is not so much as a means, but as a fruit of the abiding, that the Saviour mentions it in the parable of the Vine. He does not think so much of prayer -- as we, alas! too exclusively do -- as a means of getting blessing for ourselves, but as one of the chief channels of influence by which, through us as fellow-workers with God, the blessings of Christ's redemption are to be dispensed to the world. He sets before Himself and us the glory of the Father, in the extension of His Kingdom, as the object for which we have been made branches; and He assures us that if we but abide in Him, we shall be Israels, having power with God and man. Ours shall be the effectual, fervent prayer of the righteous man, availing much, like Elijah's for ungodly Israel. Such prayer will be the fruit of our abiding in Him, and the means of bringing forth much fruit.

To the Christian who is not abiding wholly in Jesus, the difficulties connected with prayer are often so great as to rob him of the comfort and the strength it could bring. Under the guise of humility, he asks how one so unworthy could expect to have influence with the Holy One. He thinks of God's sovereignty, His perfect wisdom and love, and cannot see how his prayer can really have any distinct effect. He prays, but it is more because he cannot rest without prayer, than from a loving faith that the prayer will be heard. But what a blessed release from such questions and perplexities is given to the soul who is truly abiding in Christ! He realizes increasingly how it is in the real spiritual unity with Christ that we are accepted and heard. The union with the Son of God is a life union: we are in very deed one with Him -- our prayer ascends as His prayer. It is because we abide in Him that we can ask what we will, and it is given to us.

There are many reasons why this must be so. One is, that abiding in Christ, and having His words abiding in us, teach us to pray in accordance with the will of God. With the abiding in Christ our self-will is kept down, the thoughts and wishes of nature are brought into captivity to the thoughts and wishes of Christ; likemindedness to Christ grows upon us -- all our working and willing become transformed into harmony with His. There is deep and oft-renewed heart-searching to see whether the surrender has indeed been entire; fervent prayer to the heart-searching Spirit that nothing may be kept back. Everything is yielded to the power of His life in us, that it may exercise its sanctifying influence even on ordinary wishes and desires. His Holy Spirit breathes through our whole being; and without our being conscious how, our desires, as the breathings of the divine life, are in conformity with the divine will, and are fulfilled. Abiding in Christ renews and sanctifies the will: we ask what we will, and it is given to us.

In close connection with this is the thought, that the abiding in Christ teaches the believer in prayer only to seek the glory of God. In promising to answer prayer, Christ's one thought (see John 14:13) is this, "that the Father may be glorified in the Son." In His intercession on earth (John 17), this was His one desire and plea; in His intercession in heaven, it is still His great object. As the believer abides in Christ, the Saviour breathes this desire into him. The thought, ONLY THE GLORY of GOD, becomes more and more the keynote of the life hid in Christ. At first this subdues, and quiets, and makes the soul almost afraid to dare entertain a wish, lest it should not be to the Father's glory. But when once its supremacy has been accepted, and everything yielded to it, it comes with mighty power to elevate and enlarge the heart, and open it to the vast field open to the glory of God. Abiding in Christ, the soul learns not only to desire, but spiritually to discern what will be for God's glory; and one of the first conditions of acceptable prayer is fulfilled in it when, as the fruit of its union with Christ, the whole mind is brought into harmony with that of the Son as He said: "Father, glorify Thy name."

130

Once more: Abiding in Christ, we can fully avail ourselves of the name of Christ. Asking in the name of another means that that other authorized me and sent me to ask, and wants to be considered as asking himself: he wants the favour done to him. Believers often try to think of the name of Jesus and His merits, and to argue themselves into the faith that they will be heard, while they painfully feel how little they have of the faith of His name. They are not living wholly in Jesus' name; it is only when they begin to pray that they want to take up that name and use it. This cannot be. The promise "Whatsoever ye ask in my name," may not be severed from the command, "Whatsoever ye do, do all in the name of the Lord Jesus." If the name of Christ is to be wholly at my disposal, so that I may have the full command of it for all I will, it must be because I first put myself wholly at His disposal, so that He has free and full command of me. It is the abiding in Christ that gives the right and power to use His name with confidence. To Christ the Father refuses nothing. Abiding in Christ, I come to the Father as one with Him. His righteousness is in me, His Spirit is in me; the Father sees the Son in me, and gives me my petition. It is not -- as so many think -- by a sort of imputation that the Father looks upon us as if we were in Christ, though we are not in Him. No; the Father wants to see us living in Him: thus shall our prayer really have power to prevail. Abiding in Christ not only renews the will to pray aright, but secures the full power of His merits to us.

Again: Abiding in Christ also works in us the faith that alone can obtain an answer. "According to your faith be it unto you": this is one of the laws of the kingdom. "Believe that ye receive, and ye shall have." This faith rests upon, and is rooted in the Word, but is something infinitely higher than the mere logical conclusion: God has promised, I shall obtain. No; faith, as a spiritual act, depends upon the words abiding in us as living powers, and so upon the state of the whole inner life. Without fasting and prayer (Mark 9:29), without humility and a spiritual mind (John 5:44), without a wholehearted obedience (1 John 3:22), there cannot be this living faith. But as the soul abides in Christ, and grows into the consciousness of its union with Him, and sees how entirely it is He who makes it and its petition acceptable, it dares to claim an answer because it knows itself one with Him. It was by faith it learnt to abide in Him; as the fruit of that faith, it rises to a larger faith in all that God has promised to be and to do. It learns to breathe its prayers in the deep, quiet, confident assurance: We know we have the petition we ask of Him.

Abiding in Christ, further, keeps us in the place where the answer can be bestowed. Some believers pray earnestly for blessing; but when God comes and looks for them to bless them, they are not to be found. They never thought that the blessing must not only be asked, but waited for, and received in prayer. Abiding in Christ is the place for receiving answers. Out of Him the answer would be dangerous -- we should consume it on our lusts (Jas. 4:3). Many of the richest answers -- say for spiritual grace, or for power to work and to bless -- can only come in the shape of a larger experience of what God makes Christ to us. The fulness is IN Him; abiding in Him is the condition of power in prayer, because the answer is treasured up and bestowed in Him.

Believer, abide in Christ, for there is the school of prayer -- mighty, effectual, answer-bringing prayer. Abide in Him, and you shall learn what to so many is a mystery: That the secret of the prayer of faith is the life of faith -- the life that abides in Christ alone.

Chapter 22 -- And In His Love

"As the Father hath loved me, so have I loved you: abide ye in my love." -- John 15:9.[1]

Blessed Lord, enlighten our eyes to see aright the glory of this wondrous word. Open to our meditation the secret chamber of THY LOVE, that our souls may enter in, and find there their everlasting dwelling-place. How else shall we know aught of a love that passeth knowledge?

Before the Saviour speaks the word that invites us to abide in His love, He first tells us what that love is. What He says of it must give force to His invitation, and make the thought of not accepting it an impossibility: "As the Father hath loved me, so I have loved you!"

"As the Father hath loved me." How shall we be able to form right conceptions of this love? Lord, teach us. God is love. Love is His very being. Love is not an attribute, but the very essence of His nature, the centre round which all His glorious attributes gather. It was because He was love that He was the Father, and that there was a Son. Love needs an object to whom it can give itself away, in whom it can lose itself, with whom it can make itself one. Because God is love, there must be a Father and a Son. The love of the Father to the Son is that divine passion with which He delights in the Son, and speaks, "My beloved Son, in whom I am well pleased." The divine love is as a burning fire; in all its intensity and infinity it has but one object and but one joy, and that is the only-begotten Son. When we gather together all the attributes of God -- His infinity, His perfection, His immensity, His majesty, His omnipotence -- and consider them but as the rays of the glory of His love, we still fail in forming any conception of what that love must be. It is a love that passeth knowledge.

And yet this love of God to His Son must serve, O my soul, as the glass in which you are to learn how Jesus loves you. As one of His redeemed ones, you are His delight, and all His desire is to you, with the longing of a love which is stronger than death, and which many waters cannot quench. His heart yearns after you, seeking your fellowship and your love. Were it needed, He could die again to possess you. As the Father loved the Son, and could not live without Him, could not be God the blessed without Him-so Jesus loves you. His life is bound up in yours; you are to Him inexpressibly more indispensable and precious than you ever can know. You are one with Himself. "As the Father hath loved me, so have I loved you." What a love!

It is an eternal love. From before the foundation of the world- God's Word teaches us this-the purpose had been formed that Christ should be the Head of His Church, that He should have a body in which His glory could be set forth. In that eternity He loved and longed for those who had been given Him by the Father; and when He came and told His disciples that He loved them, it was indeed not with a love of earth and of time, but with the love of eternity. And it is with that same infinite love that His eye still rests upon each of us here seeking to abide in Him, and in each breathing of that love there is indeed the power of eternity. "I have loved thee with an everlasting love."

It is a perfect love. It gives all, and holds nothing back. "The Father loveth the Son, and hath given all things into His hand." And just so Jesus loves His own: all He has is theirs. When it was needed, He sacrificed His throne and crown for you: He did not count His own life and blood too dear to give for you. His righteousness, His Spirit, His glory, even His throne, all are yours. This love holds nothing, nothing back, but, in a manner which no human mind can fathom, makes you one with itself. O wondrous love! to love us even as the Father loved Him, and to offer us this love as our everyday dwelling.

It is a gentle and most tender love. As we think of the love of the Father to the Son, we see in the Son everything so infinitely worthy of that love. When we think of Christ's love to us, there is nothing but sin and unworthiness to meet the eye. And the question comes: How can that love within the bosom of the divine life and its perfections be compared to the love that rests on sinners? Can it indeed be the same love? Blessed be God, we know it is so. The nature of love is always one, however different the objects. Christ knows of no other law of love but that with which His Father loved Him. Our wretchedness only serves to call out more distinctly the beauty of love, such as could not be seen even in heaven. With the tenderest compassion He bows to our weakness, with patience inconceivable He bears with our slowness, with the gentlest loving-kindness He meets our fears and our follies. It is the love of the Father to the Son, beautified, glorified, in its condescension, in its exquisite adaptation to our needs.

And it is an unchangeable love. "Having loved His own which were in the world, He loved them to the end." "The mountains shall depart, and the hills be removed, but my kindness shall not depart from thee." The promise with which it begins its work in the soul is this: "I shall not leave thee, until I have done that which I have spoken to thee of." And just as our wretchedness was what first drew it to us, so the sin, with which it is so often grieved, and which may well cause us to fear and doubt, is but a new motive for it to hold to us all the more. And why? We can give no reason but this: "As the Father hath loved me, so I have loved you."

And now, does not this love suggest the motive, the measure, and the means of that surrender by which we yield ourselves wholly to abide in Him?

This love surely supplies a motive. Only look and see how this love stands and pleads and prays. Gaze, O gaze on the divine form, the eternal glory, the heavenly beauty, the tenderly pleading gentleness of the crucified love, as it stretches out its pierced hands and says, "Oh, wilt thou not abide with me? wilt thou not come and abide in me?" It points you up to the eternity of love whence it came to seek you. It points you to the Cross, and all it has borne to prove the reality of its affection, and to win you for itself. It reminds you of all it has promised to do for you, if you will but throw yourself unreservedly into its arms. It asks you whether, so far as you have come to dwell with it and taste its blessedness, it has not done well by you. And with a divine authority, mingled with such an inexpressible tenderness that one might almost think he heard the tone of reproach in it, it says, "Soul, as the Father hath loved me, so I have loved you: abide in my love." Surely there can be but one answer to such pleading: Lord Jesus Christ! here I am. Henceforth Thy love shall be the only home of my soul: in Thy love alone will I abide.

That love is not only the motive, but also the measure, of our surrender to abide in it. Love gives all, but asks all. It does so, not because it grudges us aught, but because without this it cannot get possession of us to fill us with itself. In the love of the Father and the Son,it was so. In the love of Jesus to us, it was so. In our entering into His love to abide there, it must be so too; our surrender to it must have no other measure than its surrender to us. O that we understood how the love that calls us has infinite riches and fulness of joy for us, and that what we give up for its sake will be rewarded a hundredfold in this life! Or rather, would that we understood that it is a LOVE with a height and a depth and a length and a breadth that passes knowledge! How all thought of sacrifice or surrender would pass away, and our souls be filled with wonder at the unspeakable privilege of being loved with such a love, of being allowed to come and abide in it for ever.

And if doubt again suggest the question: But is it possible, can I always abide in His love? listen how that love itself supplies the only means for the abiding in Him: It is faith in that love which will enable us to abide in it. If this love be indeed so divine, such an intense and burning passion, then surely I can depend on it to keep me and to hold me fast. Then surely all my unworthiness and feebleness can be no hindrance. If this love be indeed so divine, with infinite power at its command, I surely have a right to trust that it is stronger than my weakness; and that with its almighty arm it will clasp me to its bosom, and suffer me to go out no more. I see how this is the one thing my God requires of me. Treating me as a reasonable being endowed with the wondrous power of willing and choosing, He cannot force all this blessedness on me, but waits till I give the willing consent of the heart. And the token of this consent He has in His great kindness ordered faith to be-that faith by which utter sinfulness casts itself into the arms of love to be saved, and utter weakness to be kept and made strong. O Infinite Love! Love with which the Father loved the Son! Love with which the Son loves us! I can trust thee, I do trust thee. O keep me abiding in Thyself.

[1] It is difficult to understand why in our English Bible one Greek word should in the first sixteen verses of John 15 have had three different translations: abide in ver. 4, continue in ver. 9, and remain in vers. 11 and 16. The Revised Version has of course kept the one word, abide.

Chapter 23 -- As Christ In The Father

"As the Father hath loved me, so I have loved you. Abide in my love, even as I abide in my Father's love."-John 15:9,10.

Christ had taught His disciples that to abide in Him was to abide in His love. The hour of His suffering is nigh, and He cannot speak much more to them. They doubtless have many questions to ask as to what that abiding in Him and His love is. He anticipates and meets their wishes, and gives them HIS OWN LIFE as the best exposition of His command. As example and rule for their abiding in His love, they have to look to His abiding in the Father's love. In the light of His union with the Father, their union with Him will become clear. His life in the Father is the law of their life in Him.

The thought is so high that we can hardly take it in, and is yet so clearly revealed, that we dare not neglect it. Do we not read in John 6 (ver.57), "As I live by the Father, even so he that eateth me, he shall live by me"? And the Saviour prays so distinctly (John 17:22), "that they may be one even as we are one: I in them, and Thou in me." The blessed union of Christ with the Father and His life in Him is the only rule of our thoughts and expectations in regard to our living and abiding in Him.

Think first of the origin of that life of Christ in the Father. They were ONE -- one in life and one in love. In this His abiding in the Father had its root. Though dwelling here on earth, He knew that He was one with the Father; that the Father's life was in Him, and His love on Him. Without this knowledge, abiding in the Father and His love would have been utterly impossible. And it is thus only that you can abide in Christ and His love. Know that you are one with Him -- one in the unity of nature. By His birth He became man, and took your nature that He might be one with you. By your new birth you become one with Him, and are made partaker of His divine nature. The link that binds you to Him is as real and close as bound Him to the Father -- the link of a divine life. Your claim on Him is as sure and always availing as was His on the Father. Your union with Him is as close.

And as it is the union of a divine life, it is one of an infinite love. In His life of humiliation on earth He tasted the blessedness and strength of knowing Himself the object of an infinite love, and of dwelling in it all the day; from His own example He invites you to learn that herein lies the secret of rest and joy. You are one with Him: yield yourself now to be loved by Him; let your eyes and heart open to the love that shines and presses in on you on every side. Abide in His love.

Think then too of the mode of that abiding in the Father and His love which is to be the law of your life. "I kept my Father's commandments and abide in His love." His was a life of subjection and dependence and yet most blessed. To our proud self-seeking nature the thought of dependence and subjection suggests the idea of humiliation and servitude; in the life of love which the Son of God lived, and to which He invite us, they are the secret of blessedness. The Son is not afraid of losing aught by giving up all to the Father, for He knows that the Father loves Him, and can have no interest apart from that of the beloved Son. He knows that as complete as is the dependence on His part is the communication on the part of the Father of all He possesses. Hence when He had said, "The Son can do nothing of Himself, except He see the Father do it," He adds at once, "Whatsoever things the Father doeth, them also doeth the Son likewise: for the Father loveth the Son, and showeth Him all things that Himself doeth." The believer who studies this life of Christ as the pattern and the promise of what his may be, learns to understand how the "Without me ye can do nothing," is but the forerunner of "I can do all things through Christ who strengtheneth me." We learn to glory in infirmities, to take pleasure in necessities and distresses for Christ's sake; for "when I am weak, then am I strong." He rises above the ordinary tone in which so many Christians speak of their weakness, while they are content to abide there, because he has learnt from Christ that in the life of divine love the emptying of self and the sacrifice of our will is the surest way to have all we can wish or will. Dependence, subjection, self-sacrifice, are for the Christian as for Christ the blessed path of life. Like as Christ lived through and in the Father, even so the believer lives through and in Christ.

Think of the glory of this life of Christ in the Father's love. Because He gave Himself wholly to the Father's will and glory, the Father crowned Him with glory and honour. He acknowledged Him as His only representative; He made Him partaker of His power and authority; He exalted Him to share His throne as God. And even so will it be with him who abides in Christ's love. If Christ finds us willing to trust ourselves and our interests to His love, if in that trust we give up all care for our own will and honour, if we make it our glory to exercise and confess absolute dependence on Him in all things, if we are content to have no life but in Him, He will do for us what the Father did for Him. He will lay of His glory on us: As the name of our Lord is Jesus is glorified in us, we are glorified in Him (2 Thess.1:12). He acknowledges us as His true and worthy representatives; He entrusts us with His power; He admits us to His counsels, as He allows our intercession to influence His rule of His Church and the world; He makes us the vehicles of His authority and His influence over men. His Spirit knows no other dwelling than such, and seeks no other instruments for His divine work. Blessed life of love for the soul that abides in Christ's love, even as He in the Father's!

Believer! abide in the love of Christ. Take and study His relation to the Father as pledge of what thine own can become. As blessed, as mighty, as glorious as was His life in the Father, can yours be in Him. Let this truth, accepted under the teaching of the Spirit in faith, remove every vestige of fear, as if abiding in Christ were a burden and a work. In the light of His life in the Father, let it henceforth be to you a blessed rest in the union with Him, an overflowing fountain of joy and strength. To abide in His love, His mighty, saving, keeping, satisfying love, even as He abode in the Father's love -- surely the very greatness of our calling teaches us that it never can be a work we have to perform; it must be with us as with Him, the result of the spontaneous outflowing of a life from within, and the mighty inworking of the love from above. What we only need is this: to take time and study the divine image of this life of love set before us in Christ. We need to have our souls still unto God, gazing upon that life of Christ in the Father until the light from heaven falls on it, and we hear the living voice of our Beloved whispering gently to us personally the teaching He gave to the disciples. Soul, be still and listen; let every thought be hushed until the word has entered your heart too: "Child! I love thee, even as the Father loved me. Abide in my love, even as I abide in the Father's love. Thy life on earth in me is to be the perfect counterpart of mine in the Father."

And if the thought will sometimes come: Surely this is too high for us; can it be really true? only remember that the greatness of the privilege is justified by the greatness of the object He has in view. Christ was the revelation of the Father on earth. He could not be this if there were not the most perfect unity, the most complete communication of all the Father had to the Son. He could be it because the Father loved Him, and He abode in that love. Believers are the revelation of Christ on earth. They cannot be this unless there be perfect unity, so that the world can know that He loves them and has sent them. But they can be it if Christ loves them with the infinite love that gives itself and all it has, and if they abide in that love.

———

143

Lord, show us Thy love. Make us with all the saints to know the love that passeth knowledge. Lord, show us in Thine own blessed life what it is to abide in Thy love. And the sight shall so win us, that it will be impossible for us one single hour to seek any other life than the life of abiding in Thy love.

Chapter 24 -- Obeying His Commandments

"If ye keep my commandments, ye shall abide in my love; even as I kept my Father's commandments, and abide in his love." -- John 15:10.

How clearly we are taught here the place which good works are to occupy in the life of the believer! Christ as the beloved Son was in the Father's love. He kept His commandments, and so He abode in the love. So the believer, without works, receives Christ and is in Him; he keeps the commandments, and so abides in the love. When the sinner, in coming to Christ, seeks to prepare himself by works, the voice of the Gospel sounds, "Not of works." When once in Christ, lest the flesh should abuse the word, "Not of works," the Gospel lifts its voice as loud: "Created in Christ Jesus unto good works" (see Eph.2:9,10). To the sinner out of Christ, works may be his greatest hindrance, keeping him from the union with the Saviour. To the believer in Christ, works are strength and blessing, for by them faith is made perfect (Jas.2:22), the union with Christ is cemented, and the soul established and more deeply rooted in the love of God. "If a man love me, he will keep my words, and my Father will love him." "If ye keep my commandments, ye shall abide in my love."

The connection between this keeping the commandments and the abiding in Christ's love is easily understood. Our union with Jesus Christ is not a thing of the intellect or sentiment, but a real vital union in heart and life. The holy life of Jesus, with His feelings and. disposition, is breathed into us by the Holy Spirit. The believer's calling is to think and feel and will just what Jesus thought and felt and willed. He desires to be partaker not only of the grace but also of the holiness of His Lord; or rather, he sees that holiness is the chief beauty of grace. To live the life of Christ means to him to be delivered from the life of self; the will of Christ is to him the only path of liberty from the slavery of his own evil self-will.

To the ignorant or slothful believer there is a great difference between the promises and commands of Scripture. The former he counts his comfort and his food; but to him who is really seeking to abide in Christ's love, the commands become no less precious, As much as the promises they are the revelation of the divine love, guides into the deeper experience of the divine life, blessed helpers in the path to a closer union with the Lord. He sees how the harmony of our will with His will is one of the chief elements of our fellowship with Him. The will is the central faculty in the Divine as in the human being. The will of God is the power that rules the whole moral as well as the natural world. How could there be fellowship with Him without delight in His will? It is only as long as salvation is to the sinner nothing but a personal safety, that he can be careless or afraid of the doing of God's will. No sooner is it to him what Scripture and the Holy Spirit reveal it to be -- the restoration to communion with God and conformity to Him -- than he feels that there is no law more natural or more beautiful than this: Keeping Christ's commandments the way to abide in Christ's love. His inmost soul approves when he hears the beloved Lord make the larger measure of the Spirit, with the manifestation of the Father and the Son in the believer, entirely dependent upon the keeping of His commandments (John 14:15,16,21,23).

There is another thing that opens to him a deeper insight and Secures a still more cordial acceptance of this truth. It is this, that in no other way did Christ Himself abide in the Father's love. In the life which Christ led upon earth, obedience was a solemn reality. The dark and awful power that led man to revolt from his God, came upon Him too, to tempt Him. To Him as man its offers of self-gratification were not matters of indifference; to refuse them, He had to fast and pray. He suffered, being tempted. He spoke very distinctly of not seeking to do His own will, as a surrender He had continually to make. He made the keeping of the Father's commandments the distinct object of His life, and so abode in His love. Does He not tell us, "I do nothing of myself, but as the Father taught me, I speak these things. And He that sent me is with me; He hath not left me alone; for I do always the things that are pleasing to Him." He thus opened to us the only path to the blessedness of a life on earth in the love of heaven; and when, as from our vine, His Spirit flows in the branches, this keeping the commands is one of the surest and highest elements of the life He inspires.

Believer! would you abide in Jesus, be very careful to keep His commandments. Keep them in the love of your heart. Be not content to have them in the Bible for reference, but have them transferred by careful study, by meditation and by prayer, by a loving acceptance, by the Spirit's teaching, to the fleshy tables of the heart. Be not content with the knowledge of some of the commands, those most commonly received among Christians, while others lie unknown and neglected. Surely, with your New Covenant privileges, you would not be behind the Old Testament saints who spoke so fervently: "I esteem all thy precepts concerning all things to be right." Be assured that there is still much of your Lord's will that you do not yet understand. Make Paul's prayer for the Colossians yours for yourself and all believers, "that you might be filled with the knowledge of His will in all wisdom and spiritual understanding"; and that of wrestling Epaphras, "that you may stand perfect and complete in all the will of God." Remember that this is one of the great elements of spiritual growth -- a deeper insight into the will of God concerning you. Imagine not that entire consecration is the end -- it is only the beginning -- of the truly holy life. See how Paul, after having (Rom. 12:1) taught believers to lay themselves upon the altar, whole and holy burnt-offerings to their God, at once proceeds (ver. 2) to tell them what the true -- altar-life is: being ever more and more "renewed in their mind to prove what is the good and perfect and acceptable will of God." The progressive renewal of the Holy Spirit leads to growing like-mindedness to Christ; then comes a delicate power of spiritual perception -- a holy instinct -- by which the soul "quick of understanding (marg. quick of scent) in the fear of the Lord," knows to recognise the meaning and the application of the Lord's commands to daily life in a way that remains hidden to the ordinary Christian. Keep them dwelling richly within you, hide them within your heart, and you shall taste the blessedness of the man whose "delight is in the law of the Lord, and in His law doth he meditate dayand night." Love will assimilate into your inmost being the commands as food from heaven. They will no longer come to you as a law standing outside and against you, but as the living power which has transformed your will into perfect harmony with all your Lord requires.

And keep them in the obedience of your life. It has been your solemn vow -- has it not? -- no longer to tolerate even a single sin: "I have sworn, and I will perform it, that I will keep Thy righteous judgments." Labour earnestly in prayer to stand perfect and complete in all the will of God. Ask earnestly for the discovery of every secret sin -- of anything that is not in perfect harmony with the will of God. Walk up to the light you have faithfully and tenderly, yielding yourself in an unreserved surrender to obey all that the Lord has spoken. When Israel took that vow (Exodus 19:8, 24:7), it was only to break it all too soon. The New Covenant gives the grace to make the vow and to keep it too (Jer.31). Be careful of disobedience even in little things. Disobedience dulls the conscience, darkens the soul, deadens our spiritual energies -- therefore keep the commandments of Christ with implicit obedience. Be a soldier that asks for nothing but the orders of the commander.

And if even for a moment the commandments appear grievous, just remember whose they are. They are the commandments of Him who loves you. They are all love, they come from His love, they lead to His love. Each new surrender to keep the commandments, each new sacrifice in keeping them, leads to deeper union with the will, the spirit, and the love of the Saviour. The double recompense of reward shall be yours -- a fuller entrance into the mystery of His love -- a fuller conformity to His own blessed life. And you shall learn to prize these words as among your choicest treasures: "If ye keep my commandments, ye shall abide in my love, EVEN AS I have kept my Father's commandments and abide in His love."

Chapter 25 -- That Your Joy May Be Full

"These things have I spoken unto you, that my joy might abide in you, and that your joy might be full." -- John 15:11

Abiding fully in Christ is a life of exquisite and overflowing happiness. As Christ gets more complete possession of the soul, it enters into the joy of its Lord. His own joy, the joy of heaven, becomes its own, and that in full measure, and as an ever-abiding portion. Just as joy on earth is everywhere connected with the vine and its fruit, so joy is an essential characteristic of the life of the believer who fully abides in Christ, the heavenly Vine.

We all know the value of joy. It alone is the proof that what we have really satisfies the heart. As long as duty, or self-interest, or other motives influence me, men cannot know what the object of my pursuit or possession is really worth to me. But when it gives me joy, and they see me delight in it, they know that to me at least it is a treasure. Hence there is nothing so attractive as joy, no preaching so persuasive as the sight of hearts made glad. Just this makes gladness such a mighty element in the Christian character: there is no proof of the reality of God's love and the blessing He bestows, which men so soon feel the force of, as when the joy of God overcomes all the trials of life. And for the Christian's own welfare, joy is no less indispensable: the joy of the Lord is his strength; confidence, and courage, and patience find their inspiration in joy. With a heart full of joy no work can weary, and no burden can depress; God Himself is strength and song.

Let us hear what the Saviour says of the joy of abiding in Him. He promises us His own joy: "My joy." As the whole parable refers to the life His disciples should have in Him when ascended to heaven, the joy is that of His resurrection life. This is clear from those other words of His (John 16:22): "I will see you again, and your heart shall rejoice, and your joy shall no man take from you." It was only with the resurrection and its glory that the power of the never-changing life began, and only in it that the never-ceasing joy could have its rise. With it was fulfilled the word: "Therefore thy God hath anointed thee with the oil of gladness above thy fellows." The day of His crowning was the day of the gladness of His heart. That joy of His was the joy of a work fully and for ever completed, the joy of the Father's bosom regained, and the joy of souls redeemed. These are the elements of His joy; of them the abiding in Him makes us partakers. The believer shares so fully His victory and His perfect redemption, that his faith can without ceasing sing the conqueror's song: "Thanks be to God, who always causeth me to triumph." As the fruit of this, there is the joy of the undisturbed dwelling in the light of the Father's love -- not a cloud to intervene if the abiding be unbroken. And then, with this joy in the love of the Father, as a love received, the joy of the love of souls, as love going out and rejoicing over the lost. Abiding in Christ, penetrating into the very depths of His life and heart, seeking for the most perfect oneness, these the three streams of His joy flow into our hearts. Whether we look backward and see the work He has done, or upward and see the reward He has in the Father's love that passeth knowledge, or forward in the continual accessions of joy as sinners are brought home, His joy is ours. With our feet on Calvary, our eyes on the Father's countenance, and our hands helping sinners home, we have His joy as our own.

And then He speaks of this joy as abiding -- a joy that is never to cease or to be interrupted for a moment: "That my joy might abide in you." "Your joy no man taketh from you." This is what many Christians cannot understand. Their view of the Christian life is that it is a succession of changes, now joy and now sorrow. And they appeal to the experiences of a man like the Apostle Paul, as a proof of how much there may be of weeping, and sorrow, and suffering. They have not noticed how just Paul gives the strongest evidence as to this unceasing joy. He understood the paradox of the Christian life as the combination at one and the same moment of all the bitterness of earth and all the joy of heaven. "As sorrowful, yet always rejoicing": these precious golden words teach us how the joy of Christ can overrule the sorrow of the world, can make us sing while we weep, and can maintain in the heart, even when cast down by disappointment or difficulties, a deep consciousness of a joy that is unspeakable and full of glory. There is but one condition: "I will see you again, and your heart shall rejoice, and your joy shall no man take from you." The presence of Jesus, distinctly manifested, cannot but give joy. Abiding in Him consciously, how can the soul but rejoice and be glad? Even when weeping for the sins and the souls of others, there is the fountain of gladness springing up in the faith of His power and love to save.

And this His own joy abiding with us, He wants to be full. Of the full joy our Saviour spoke thrice on the last night. Once here in the parable of the Vine: "These things have I spoken unto you that your joy might be full"; and every deeper insight into the wonderful blessedness of being the branch of such a Vine confirms His Word. Then He connects it (John 16:24) with our prayers being answered: "Ask and ye shall receive, that your joy may be full." To the spiritual mind, answered prayer is not only a means of obtaining certain blessings, but something infinitely higher. It is a token of our fellowship with the Father and the Son in heaven, of their delight in us, and our having been admitted and having had a voice in that wondrous interchange of love in which the Father and the Son hold counsel, and decide the daily guidance of the children on earth. To a soul abiding in Christ, that longs for manifestations of His love, and that understands to take an answer to prayer in its true spiritual value, as a response from the throne to all its utterances of love and trust, the joy which it brings is truly unutterable. The word is found true: "Ask and ye shall receive, and your joy shall be full." And then the Saviour says, in His highpriestly prayer to the Father (John 17:13), "These things I speak, that they might have my joy fulfilled in themselves." It is the sight of the great High Priest entering the Father's presence for us, ever living to pray and carry on His blessed work in the power of an endless life, that removes every possible cause of fear or doubt, and gives us the assurance and experience of a perfect salvation. Let the believer who seeks, according to the teaching of John 15, to possess the full joy of abiding in Christ, and according to John 16, the full joy of prevailing prayer, press forward to John 17. Let him there listen to those wondrous words of intercession spoken, that his joy might be full. Let him, as he listens to those words, learn the love that even now pleads for him in heaven without ceasing, the glorious objects for which it is pleading, and which through its all-prevailing pleading are hourly being realized, and Christ's joy will be fulfilled in him.

Christ's own joy, abiding joy, fulness of joy -- such is the portion of the believer who abides in Christ. Why, O why is it that this joy has so little power to attract? The reason simply is: Men, yea, even God's children, do not believe in it. Instead of the abiding in Christ being looked upon as the happiest life that ever can be led, it is regarded as a life of self-denial and of sadness. They forget that the self-denial and the sadness are owing to the not abiding, and that to those who once yield themselves unreservedly to abide in Christ as a bright and blessed life, their faith comes true -- the joy of the Lord is theirs. The difficulties all arise from the want of the full surrender to a full abiding.

Child of God, who seekest to abide in Christ, remember what the Lord says. At the close of the parable of the Vine He adds these precious words: "These things have I spoken unto you, that my joy might abide in you, and that your joy might be full." Claim the joy as part of the branch life -- not the first or chief part, but as the blessed proof of the sufficiency of Christ to satisfy every need of the soul. Be happy. Cultivate gladness. If there are times when it comes of itself, and the heart feels the unutterable joy of the Saviour's presence, praise God for it, and seek to maintain it. If at other times feelings are dull, and the experience of the joy not such as you could wish it, still praise God for the life of unutterable blessedness to which you have been redeemed. In this, too, the word holds good: "According to your faith be it unto you." As you claim all the other gifts in Jesus, ever claim this one too -- not for your own sake, but for His and the Father's glory. "My joy in you"; "that my joy may abide in you"; "my joy fulfilled in themselves" -- these are Jesus' own words. It is impossible to take Him wholly and heartily, and not to get His joy too. Therefore, "Rejoice in the Lord alway; and again I say, Rejoice."

Chapter 26 -- And In Love To The Brethren

"This is my commandment, That ye love one another, as I have loved you." -- John 15:12.

"Like as the Father loved me, EVEN so I have loved you; LIKE AS I have loved you, EVEN SO love ye one another." God became man; divine love began to run in the channel of a human heart; it becomes the love of man to man. The love that fills heaven and eternity is ever to be daily seen here in the life of earth and of time.

"This is my commandment," the Saviour says, "That ye love one another, as I have loved you." He sometimes spoke of commandments, but the love, which is the fulfilling of the law, is the all-including one, and therefore is called His commandment -- the new commandment. It is to be the great evidence of the reality of the New Covenant, of the power of the new life revealed in Jesus Christ. It is to be the one convincing and indisputable token of discipleship: "Hereby shall all men know that ye are my disciples"; "That they may be one in us, that the world may believe"; "That they may be made perfect in one, that the world may know that Thou hast loved them, as Thou hast loved me." To the believer seeking perfect fellowship with Christ, the keeping of this commandment is at once the blessed proof that he is abiding in Him, and the path to a fuller and more perfect union.

Let us try to understand how this is so. We know that God is love, and that Christ came to reveal this, not as a doctrine but as a life. His life, in its wonderful self-abasement and self-sacrifice, was, above everything, the embodiment of divine love, the showing forth to men, in such human manifestations as they could understand, how God loves. In His love to the unworthy and the ungrateful, in His humbling Himself to walk among men as a servant, in His giving Himself up to death, He simply lived and acted out the life of the divine love which was in the heart of God. He lived and died to show us the love of the Father.

And now, just as Christ was to show forth God's love, believers are to show forth to the world the love of Christ. They are to prove to men that Christ loves them, and in loving fills them with a love that is not of earth. They, by living and by loving just as He did, are to be perpetual witnesses to the love that gave itself to die. He loved so that even the Jews cried out, as at Bethany, "Behold how He loved!" Christians are to live so that men are compelled to say, "See how these Christians love one another." In their daily intercourse with each other, Christians are made a spectacle to God, and to angels, and to men; and in the Christlikeness of their love to each other, are to prove what manner of spirit they are of. Amid all diversity of character or of creed, of language or of station, they are to prove that love has made them members of one body, and of each other, and has taught them each to forget and sacrifice self for the sake of the other. Their life of love is the chief evidence of Christianity, the proof to the world that God sent Christ, and that He has shed abroad in them the same love with which He loved Him. Of all the evidences of Christianity, this is the mightiest and most convincing.

This love of Christ's disciples to each other occupies a central position between their love to God and to all men. Of their love to God, whom they cannot see, it is the test. The love to one unseen may so easily be a mere sentiment, or even an imagination; in the intercourse with God's children, love to God is really called into exercise, and shows itself in deeds that the Father accepts as done to Himself. So alone can it be proved to be true. The love to the brethren is the flower and fruit of the root, unseen in the heart, of love to God. And this fruit again becomes the seed of love to all men: intercourse with each other is the school in which believers are trained and strengthened to love their fellow-men, who are yet out of Christ, not simply with the liking that rests on points of agreement, but with the holy love that takes hold of the unworthiest, and bears with the most disagreeable for Jesus' sake. It is love to each other as disciples that is ever put in the foreground as the link between love to God alone and to men in general.

In Christ's intercourse with His disciples this brotherly love finds the law of its conduct. As it studies His forgiveness and forbearance towards His friends, with the seven times seven as its only measure -- as it looks to His unwearied patience and His infinite humility -- as it sees the meekness and lowliness with which He seeks to win for Himself a place as their servant, wholly devoted to their interests -- it accepts with gladness His command, "Ye should do as I have done" (John 13:15). Following His example, each lives not for Himself but for the other. The law of kindness is on the tongue, for love has vowed that never shall one unkind word cross its lips. It refuses not only to speak, but even to hear or to think evil; of the name and character of the fellow-Christian it is more jealous than of its own. My own good name I may leave to the Father; my brother's my Father has entrusted to me. In gentleness and loving kindness, in courtesy and generosity, in self-sacrifice and beneficence, in its life of blessing and of beauty, the divine love, which has been shed abroad in the believer's heart, shines out as it shone in the life of Jesus.

Christian! what say you of this your glorious calling to love like Christ? Does not your heart bound at the thought of the unspeakable privilege of thus showing forth the likeness of the Eternal Love? Or are you rather ready to sigh at the thought of the inaccessible height of perfection to which you are thus called to climb? Brother, sigh not at what is in very deed the highest token of the Father's love, that He has called us to be like Christ in our love, just as He was like the Father in His love. Understand that He who gave the command in such close connection with His teaching about the Vine and the abiding in Him, gave us in that the assurance that we have only to abide in Him to be able to love like Him. Accept the command as a new motive to a more full abiding in Christ. Regard the abiding in Him more than ever as an abiding in His love; rooted and grounded daily in a love that passeth knowledge, you receive of its fulness, and learn to love. With Christ abiding in you, the Holy Spirit sheds abroad the love of God in your heart, and you love the brethren, the most trying and unloveable, with a love that is not your own, but the love of Christ in you. And the command about your love to the brethren is changed from a burden into a joy, if you but keep it linked, as Jesus linked it, to the command about His love to you: "Abide in my love; love one another, as I have loved you."

"This is my commandment, That ye love one another, as I have loved you." Is not this now some of the much fruit that Jesus has promised we shall bear -- in very deed a cluster of the grapes of Eshcol, with which we can prove to others that the land of promise is indeed a good land? Let us try in all simplicity and honesty to go out to our home to translate the language of high faith and heavenly enthusiasm into the plain prose of daily conduct, so that all men can understand it. Let our temper be under the rule of the love of Jesus: He can not alone curb it -- He can make us gentle and patient. Let the vow, that not an unkind word about others shall ever be heard from our lips, be laid trustingly at His feet. Let the gentleness that refuses to take offence, that is always ready to excuse, to think and hope the best, mark our intercourse with all. Let the love that seeks not its own, but ever is ready to wash others' feet, or even to give its life for them, be our aim as we abide in Jesus. Let our life be one of self-sacrifice, always studying the welfare of others, finding our highest joy in blessing others. And let us, in studying the divine art of doing good, yield ourselves as obedient learners to the guidance of the Holy Spirit. By His grace, the most commonplace life can be transfigured with the brightness of a heavenly beauty, as the infinite love of the divine nature shines out through our frail humanity. Fellow-Christian, let us praise God! We are called to love as Jesus loves, as God loves.

"Abide in my love, and love as I have loved." Bless God, it is possible. The new holy nature we have, and which grows ever stronger as it abides in Christ the Vine, can love as He did. Every discovery of the evil of the old nature, every longing desire to obey the command of our Lord, every experience of the power and the blessedness of loving with Jesus' love, will urge us to accept with fresh faith the blessed injunctions: "Abide in me, and I in you"; "Abide in my love."

161

Chapter 27 -- That You May Not Sin

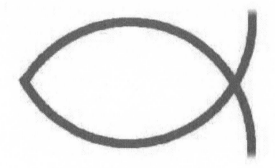

"In him is no sin. Whosoever abideth in him sinneth not." -- 1 John 3:5,6.

"Ye know," the apostle had said, "that He was manifested to take away our sin," and had thus indicated salvation from sin as the great object for which the Son was made man. The connection shows clearly that the taking away has reference not only to the atonement and freedom from guilt, but to deliverance from the power of sin, so that the believer no longer does it. It is Christ's personal holiness that constitutes His power to effect this purpose. He admits sinners into life union with Himself; the result is, that their life becomes like His. "In Him is no sin. Whosoever abideth in Him sinneth not." As long as he abides, and as far as he abides, the believer does not sin. Our holiness of life has its roots in the personal holiness of Jesus. "If the root be holy, so also are the branches."

The question at once arises: How is this consistent with what the Bible teaches of the abiding corruption of our human nature, or with what John himself tells of the utter falsehood of our profession, if we say that we have no sin, that we have not sinned? (see I John 1:8,10). It is just this passage which, if we look carefully at it, will teach us to understand our text aright. Note the difference in the two statements (ver. 8), "If we say that we have no sin," and (ver.10), "If we say that we have not sinned." The two expressions cannot be equivalent; the second would then be an unmeaning repetition of the first. Having sin in verse 8 is not the same as doing sin in verse 10. Having sin is having a sinful nature. The holiest believer must each moment confess that he has sin within him -- the flesh, namely, in which dwelleth no good thing. Sinning or doing sin is something very different: it is yielding to indwelling sinful nature, and falling into actual transgression. And so we have two admissions that every true believer must make. The one is that he has still sin within him (ver. 8); the second, that that sin has in former times broken out into sinful actions (ver.10). No believer can say either, "I have no sin in me," or "I have in time past never sinned." If we say we have no sin at present, or that we have not sinned in the past, we deceive ourselves. But no confession, though we have sin in the present, is demanded that we are doing sin in the present too; the confession of actual sinning refers to the past. It may, as appears from chapter 2:2, be in the present also, but is expected not to be. And so we see how the deepest confession of sin in the past (as Paul's of his having been a persecutor), and the deepest consciousness of having still a vile and corrupt nature in the present, may consist with humble but joyful praise to Him who keeps from stumbling.

But how is it possible that a believer, having sin in him -- sin of such intense vitality, and such terrible power as we know the flesh to have -- that a believer having sin should yet not be doing sin? The answer is: "In Him is no sin. He that abideth in Him sinneth not." When the abiding in Christ becomes close and unbroken, so that the soul lives from moment to moment in the perfect union with the Lord its keeper, He does, indeed, keep down the power of the old nature, so that it does not regain dominion over the soul. We have seen that there are degrees in the abiding. With most Christians the abiding is so feeble and intermittent, that sin continually obtains the ascendency, and brings the soul into subjection. The divine promise given to faith is: "Sin shall not have dominion over you." But with the promise is the command: "Let not sin reign in your mortal body." The believer who claims the promise in full faith has the power to obey the command, and sin is kept from asserting its supremacy. Ignorance of the promise, or unbelief, or unwatchfulness, opens the door for sin to reign. And so the life of many believers is a course of continual stumbling and sinning. But when the believer seeks full admission into, and a permanent abode in Jesus, the Sinless One, then the life of Christ keeps from actual transgression. "In Him is no sin. He that abideth in Him sinneth not. " Jesus does indeed save him from his sin -- not by the removal of his sinful nature, but by keeping him from yielding to it.

I have read of a young lion whom nothing could awe or keep down but the eye of his keeper. With the keeper you could come near him, and he would crouch, his savage nature all unchanged, and thirsting for blood -- trembling at the keeper's feet. You might put your foot on his neck, as long as the keeper was with you. To approach him without the keeper would be instant death. And so it is that the believer can have sin and yet not do sin. The evil nature, the flesh, is unchanged in its enmity against God, but the abiding presence of Jesus keeps it down. In faith the believer entrusts himself to the keeping, to the indwelling, of the Son of God; he abides in Him, and counts on Jesus to abide in Him too. The union and fellowship is the secret of a holy life: "In Him is no sin; he that abideth in Him sinneth not."

And now another question will arise: Admitted that the complete abiding in the Sinless One will keep from sinning, is such abiding possible? May we hope to be able so to abide in Christ, say, even for one day, that we may be kept from actual transgressions? The question has only to be fairly stated and considered -- it will suggest its own answer. When Christ commanded us to abide in Him, and promised us such rich fruit-bearing to the glory of the Father, and such mighty power in our intercessions, can He have meant anything but the healthy, vigorous, complete union of the branch with the vine? When He promised that as we abide in Him He would abide in us, could He mean anything but that His dwelling in us would be a reality of divine power and love? Is not this way of saving from sin just that which will glorify Him? -- keeping us daily humble and helpless in the consciousness of the evil nature, watchful and active in the knowledge of its terrible power, dependent and trustful in the remembrance that only His presence can keep the lion down. O let us believe that when Jesus said, "Abide in me, and I in you," He did indeed mean that, while we were not to be freed from the world and its tribulation, from the sinful nature and its temptations, we were at least to have this blessing fully secured to us -- grace to abide wholly, only, even in our Lord. The abiding in Jesus makes it possible to keep from actual sinning; and Jesus Himself makes it possible to abide in Him.

Beloved Christian! I do not wonder if the promise of the text appears almost too high. Do not, I pray, let your attention be diverted by the question as to whether it would be possible to be kept for your whole life, or for so many years, without sinning. Faith has ever only to deal with the present moment. Ask this: Can Jesus at the present moment, as I abide in Him, keep me from those actual transgressions which have been the stain and the weariness of my daily life? You cannot but say: Surely He can. Take Him then at this present moment, and say, "Jesus keeps me now, Jesus saves me now." Yield yourself to Him in the earnest and believing prayer to be kept abiding, by His own abiding in you -- and go into the next moment, and the succeeding hours, with this trust continually renewed. As often as the opportunity occurs in the moments between your occupations, renew your faith in an act of devotion: Jesus keeps me now, Jesus saves me now. Let failure and sin, instead of discouraging you, only urge you still more to seek your safety in abiding in the Sinless One. Abiding is a grace in which you can grow wonderfully, if you will but make at once the complete surrender, and then persevere with ever larger expectations. Regard it as His work to keep you abiding in Him, and His work to keep you from sinning. It is indeed your work to abide in Him; but it is that, only because it is His work as Vine to bear and hold the branch. Gaze upon His holy human nature as what He prepared for you to be partaker of with Himself, and you will see that there is something even higher and better than being kept from sin -- that is but the restraining from evil: there is the positive and larger blessing of being now a vessel purified and cleansed, of being filled with His fulness, and made the channel of showing forth His power, His blessing, and His glory.

NOTE
Is Daily Sinning An Inevitable Necessity?

"Why is it that, when we possess a Saviour whose love and lower are infinite, we are so often filled with fear and despondency? We are wearied and faint in our minds, because we do not look stedfastly unto Jesus, the author and finisher of faith, who is set down at the right hand of God -- unto Him whose omnipotence embraces both heaven and earth, who is strong and mighty in His feeble saints.

"While we remember our weakness, we forget His all-sufficient power. While we acknowledge that apart from Christ we can do nothing, we do not rise to the height or depth of Christian humility: I can do all things through Christ which strengtheneth me. While we trust in the power of the death of Jesus to cancel the guilt of sin, we do not exercise a reliant and appropriating faith in the omnipotence of the living Saviour to deliver us from the bondage and power of sin in our daily life. We forget that Christ worketh in us mightily, and that, one with Him, we possess strength sufficient to overcome every temptation. We are apt either to forget our nothingness, and imagine that in our daily path we can live without sin, that the duties and trials of our everyday life can be performed and borne in our own strength; or we do not avail ourselves of the omnipotence of Jesus, who is able to subdue all things to Himself, and to keep us from the daily infirmities and falls which we are apt to imagine an inevitable necessity. If we really depended in all things and at all times on Christ, we would in all things and at all times gain the victory through Him whose power is infinite, and who is appointed by the Father to be the Captain of our salvation. Then all our deeds would be wrought, not merely before, but in God. We would then do all things to the glory of the Father, in the all-powerful name of Jesus, who is our sanctification. Remember that unto Him all power is given in heaven and on earth, and live by the constant exercise of faith in His power. Let us most fully believe that we have and are nothing, that with man it is impossible, that in ourselves we have no life which can bring forth fruit; but that Christ is all -- that abiding in Him, and His word dwelling in us, we can bring forth fruit to the glory of the Father" -- From Christ and the Church. Sermons by Adolph Saphir. The italics are not in the original.

Chapter 28 -- As Your Strength

"All power is given UNTO ME in heaven and in earth." -- Matt.28:18. [1]
"Be strong IN THE LORD, and in the power of his might." -- Eph.6.10.
"My power is made perfect in weakness." -- 2 Cor.12:9 (R.V.).

There is no truth more generally admitted among earnest Christians than that of their utter weakness. There is no truth more generally misunderstood and abused. Here, as elsewhere, God's thoughts are heaven-high above man's thoughts.

The Christian often tries to forget his weakness: God wants us to remember it, to feel it deeply. The Christian wants to conquer his weakness and to be freed from it: God wants us to rest and even rejoice in it. The Christian mourns over his weakness: Christ teaches His servant to say, "I take pleasure in infirmities; most gladly will I glory in my infirmities." The Christian thinks his weakness his greatest hindrance in the life and service of God: God tells us that it is the secret of strength and success. It is our weakness, heartily accepted and continually realized, that gives us our claim and access to the strength of Him who has said, "My strength is made perfect in weakness."

When our Lord was about to take His seat upon the throne, one of His last words was: "All power is given unto me in heaven and on earth." Just as His taking His place at the right hand of the power of God was something new and true -- a real advance in the history of the God-man -- so was this clothing with all power. Omnipotence was now entrusted to the man Christ Jesus, that from henceforth through the channels of human nature it might put forth its mighty energies. Hence He connected with this revelation of what He was to receive, the promise of the share that His disciples would have in it: When I am ascended, ye shall receive power from on high (Luke 24:49; Acts 1:8). It is in the power of the omnipotent Saviour that the believer must find his strength for life and for work.

It was thus with the disciples. During ten days they worshipped and waited at the footstool of His throne. They gave expression to their faith in Him as their Saviour, to their adoration of Him as their Lord, to their love to Him as their Friend, to their devotion and readiness to work for Him as their Master. Jesus Christ was the one object of thought, of love, of delight. In such worship of faith and devotion their souls grew up into intensest communion with Him upon the throne, and when they were prepared, the baptism of power came. It was power within and power around.

The power came to qualify for the work to which they had yielded themselves -- of testifying by life and word to their unseen Lord. With some the chief testimony was to be that of a holy life, revealing the heaven and the Christ from whom it came. The power came to set up the Kingdom within them, to give them the victory over sin and self, to fit them by living experience to testify to the power of Jesus on the throne, to make men live in the world as saints. Others were to give themselves up entirely to the speaking in the name of Jesus. But all needed and all received the gift of power, to prove that now Jesus had received the Kingdom of the Father, all power in heaven and earth was indeed given to Him, and by Him imparted to His people just as they needed it, whether for a holy life or effective service. They received the gift of power, to prove to the world that the Kingdom of God, to which they professed to belong, was not in word but in power. By having power within, they had power without and around. The power of God was felt even by those who would not yield themselves to it (Acts 2.43; 4:13; 5:13).

And what Jesus was to these first disciples, He is to us too. Our whole life and calling as disciples find their origin and their guarantee in the words: "All power is given to me in heaven and on earth." What He does in and through us, He does with almighty power. What He claims or demands, He works Himself by that same power. All He gives, He gives with power. Every blessing He bestows, every promise He fulfils, every grace He works -- all, all is to be with power. Everything that comes from this Jesus on the throne of power is to bear the stamp of power. The weakest believer may be confident that in asking to be kept from sin, to grow in holiness, to bring forth much fruit, be may count upon these his petitions being fulfilled with divine power. The power is in Jesus; Jesus is ours with all His fulness; it is in us His members that the power is to work and be made manifest.

And if we want to know how the power is bestowed, the answer is simple: Christ gives His power in us by giving His life in us. He does not, as so many believers imagine, take the feeble life He finds in them, and impart a little strength to aid them in their feeble efforts. No; it is in giving His own life in us that He gives us His power. The Holy Spirit came down to the disciples direct from the heart of their exalted Lord, bringing down into them the glorious life of heaven into which He had entered. And so His people are still taught to be strong in the Lord and in the power of His might. When He strengthens them, it is not by taking away the sense of feebleness, and giving in its place the feeling of strength. By no means. But in a very wonderful way leaving and even increasing the sense of utter impotence, He gives them along with it the consciousness of strength in Him. "We have this treasure in earthen vessels, that the excellency of the power may be of God and not of us." The feebleness and the strength are side by side; as the one grows, the other too, until they understand the saying, "When I am weak, then am I strong; I glory in my infirmities, that the power of Christ may rest on me."

The believing disciple learns to look upon Christ on the throne, Christ the Omnipotent, as his life. He studies that life in its infinite perfection and purity, in its strength and glory; it is the eternal life dwelling in a glorified man. And when he thinks of his own inner life, and longs for holiness, to live wellpleasing unto God, or for power to do the Father's work, he looks up, and, rejoicing that Christ is his life, he confidently reckons that that life will work mightily in him all he needs. In things little and things great, in the being kept from sin from moment to moment for which he has learned to look, or in the struggle with some special difficulty or temptation, the power of Christ is the measure of his expectation. He lives a most joyous and blessed life, not because he is no longer feeble, but because, being utterly helpless, he consents and expects to have the mighty Saviour work in him.

The lessons these thoughts teach us for practical life are simple, but very precious. The first is, that all our strength is in Christ, laid up and waiting for use. It is there as an almighty life, which is in Him for us, ready to flow in according to the measure in which it finds the channels open. But whether its flow is strong or feeble, whatever our experience of it be, there it is in Christ: All power in heaven and earth. Let us take time to study this. Let us get our minds filled with the thought: That Jesus might be to us a perfect Saviour, the Father gave Him all power. That is the qualification that fits Him for our needs: All the power of heaven over all the powers of earth, over every power of earth in our heart and life too.

The second lesson is: This power flows into us as we abide in close union with Him. When the union is feeble, little valued or cultivated, the inflow of strength will be feeble. When the union with Christ is rejoiced in as our highest good, and everything sacrificed for the sake of maintaining it, the power will work: "His strength will be made perfect in our weakness." Our one care must therefore be to abide in Christ as our strength. Our one duty is to be strong in the Lord,and in the power of His might. Let our faith cultivate large and clear apprehensions of the exceeding greatness of God's power in them that believe, even that power of the risen and exalted Christ by which He triumphed over every enemy (Eph. 1: 19-21). Let our faith consent to God's wonderful and most blessed arrangement: nothing but feebleness in us as our own, all the power in Christ, and yet within our reach as surely as if it were in us. Let our faith daily go out of self and its life into the life of Christ, placing our whole being at His disposal for Him to work in us. Let our faith, above all, confidently rejoice in the assurance that He will in very deed, with His almighty power, perfect His work in us. As we thus abide in Christ, the Holy Spirit, the Spirit of His power, will work mightily in us, and we too shall sing, "JEHOVAH is my strength and song: IN JEHOVAH I have righteousness and strength." "I can do all things through Christ, which strengtheneth me."

[1] The word power in this verse is properly authority (R.V.), but the two ideas are so closely linked, and the authority as a living divine reality is so inseparable from the power, that I have felt at liberty to retain the word power.

Chapter 29 -- And Not In Self

"In me, that is, in my flesh, dwelleth no good thing." -- Rom. 7:18.

To have life in Himself is the prerogative of God alone, and of the Son, to whom the Father hath also given it. To seek life, not in itself, but in God, is the highest honour of the creature. To live in and to himself is the folly and guilt of sinful man; to live to God in Christ, the blessedness of the believer. To deny, to hate, to forsake, to lose his own life, such is the secret of the life of faith. "I live, yet NOT I, but Christ liveth in me"; "NOT I, but the grace of God which is with me": this is the testimony of each one who has found out what it is to give up his own life, and to receive instead the blessed life of Christ within us. There is no path to true life, to abiding in Christ, than that which our Lord went before us -- through death.

At the first commencement of the Christian life, but few see this. In the joy of pardon, they feel constrained to live for Christ, and trust with the help of God to be enabled to do so. They are as yet ignorant of the terrible enmity of the flesh against God, and its absolute refusal in the believer to be subject to the law of God. They know not yet that nothing but death, the absolute surrender to death of all that is of nature, will suffice, if the life of God is to be manifested in them with power. But bitter experience of failure soon teaches them the insufficiency of what they have yet known of Christ's power to save, and deep heart-longings are awakened to know Him better. He lovingly points them to His cross. He tells them that as there, in the faith of His death as their substitute, they found their title to life, so there they shall enter into its fuller experience too. He asks them if they are indeed willing to drink of the cup of which He drank -- to be crucified and to die with Him. He teaches them that in Him they are indeed already crucified and dead -- all unknowing, at conversion they became partakers of His death. But what they need now is to give a full and intelligent consent to what they received ere they understood it, by an act of their own choice to will to die with Christ.

This demand of Christ's is one of unspeakable solemnity. Many a believer shrinks back from it. He can hardly understand it. He has become so accustomed to a low life of continual stumbling, that he hardly desires, and still less expects, deliverance. Holiness, perfect conformity to Jesus, unbroken fellowship with His love, can scarcely be counted distinct articles of his creed. Where there is not intense longing to be kept to the utmost from sinning, and to be brought into the closest possible union with the Saviour, the thought of being crucified with Him can find no entrance. The only impression it makes is that of suffering and shame: such a one is content that Jesus bore the cross, and so won for him the crown he hopes to wear. How different the light in which the believer who is really seeking to abide fully in Christ looks upon it. Bitter experience has taught him how, both in the matter of entire surrender and simple trust, his greatest enemy in the abiding life, is SELF. Now it refuses to give up its will; then again, by its working, it hinders God's work. Unless this life of self, with its willing and working, be displaced by the life of Christ, with His willing and working, to abide in Him will be impossible. And then comes the solemn question from Him who died on the cross: "Are you ready to give up self to the death?" You yourself, the living person born of God, are already in me dead to sin and alive to God; but are you ready now, in the power of this death, to mortify your members, to give up self entirely to its death of the cross, to be kept there until it be wholly destroyed? The question is a heart-searching one. Am I prepared to say that the old self shall no longer have a word to say; that it shall not be allowed to have a single thought, however natural -- not a single feeling, however gratifying -- not a single wish or work, however right?

Is this in very deed what He requires? Is not our nature God's handiwork, and may not our natural powers be sanctified to His service? They may and must indeed. But perhaps you have not yet seen how the only way they can be sanctified is that they be taken from under the power of self, and brought under the power of the life of Christ. Think not that this is a work that you can do, because you earnestly desire it, and are indeed one of His redeemed ones. No, there is no way to the altar of consecration but through death. As you yielded yourself a sacrifice on God's altar as one alive from the dead (Rom.6:13, 7:1), so each power of your nature -- each talent, gift, possession, that is really to be holiness to the Lord -- must be separated from the power of sin and self, and laid on the altar to be consumed by the fire that is ever burning there. It is in the mortifying, the slaying of self, that the wonderful powers with which God has fitted you to serve Him, can be set free for a complete surrender to God, and offered to Him to be accepted, and sanctified, and used. And though, as long as you are in the flesh, there is no thought of being able to say that self is dead, yet when the life of Christ is allowed to take full possession, self can be so kept in its crucifixion place, and under its sentence of death, that it shall have ho dominion over you, not for a single moment. Jesus Christ becomes your second self.

Believer! would you truly and fully abide in Christ, prepare yourself to part for ever from self, and not to allow it, even for a single moment, to have aught to say in your inner life. If you are willing to come entirely away out of self, and to allow Jesus Christ to become your life within you, inspiring all your thinking, feeling, acting, in things temporal and spiritual, He is ready to undertake the charge. In the fullest and widest sense the word life ever can have, He will be your life, extending His interest and influence to each one, even the minutest, of the thousand things that make up your daily life. To do this He asks but one thing: Come away out of self and its life, abide in Christ and the Christ life, and Christ will be your life. The power of His holy presence will cast out the old life.

To this end give up self at once and for ever. If you have never yet dared to do it, for fear you might fail of your engagement, do it now, in view of the promise Christ gives you that His life will take the place of the old life. Try and realize that though self is not dead, you are indeed dead to self. Self is still strong and living, but it has no power over you. You, your renewed nature -- you, your new self, begotten again in Jesus Christ from the dead -- are indeed dead to sin and alive to God. Your death in Christ has freed you completely from the control of self: it has no power over you, except as you, in ignorance, or unwatchfulness, or unbelief, consent to yield to its usurped authority. Come and accept by faith simply and heartily the glorious position you have in Christ. As one who, in Christ, has a life dead to self, as one who is freed from the dominion of self, and has received His divine life to take the place of self, to be the animating and inspiring principle of your life, venture boldly to plant the foot upon the neck of this enemy of yours and your Lord's. Be of good courage, only believe; fear not to take the irrevocable step, and to say that you have once for all given up self to the death for which it has been crucified in Christ (Rom.6:6). And trust Jesus the Crucified One to hold self to the cross, and to fill its place in you with His own blessed resurrection life.

In this faith, abide in Christ! Cling to Him; rest on Him; hope on Him. Daily renew your consecration; daily accept afresh your position as ransomed from your tyrant, and now in turn made a conqueror. Daily look with holy fear on the enemy, self, struggling to get free from the cross, seeking to allure you into giving it some little liberty, or else ready to deceive you by its profession of willingness now to do service to Christ. Remember, self seeking to serve God is more dangerous than self refusing obedience. Look upon it with holy fear, and hide yourself in Christ: in Him alone is your safety. Abide thus in Him; He has promised to abide in you. He will teach you to be humble and watchful. He will teach you to be happy and trustful. Bring every interest of your life, every power of your nature, all the unceasing flow of thought, and will, and feeling, that makes up life, and trust Him to take the place that self once filled so easily and so naturally. Jesus Christ will indeed take possession of you and dwell in you; and in the restfulness and peace and grace of the new life you shall have unceasing joy at the wondrous exchange that has been made -- the coming out of self to abide in Christ alone.

NOTE

In his work on Sanctification, Marshall, in the twelfth chapter, on "Holiness through faith alone," puts with great force the danger in which the Christian is of seeking sanctification in the power of the flesh, with the help of Christ, instead of looking for it to Christ alone, and receiving it from Him by faith. He reminds us how there are two natures in the believer, and so two ways of seeking holiness, according as we allow the principles of the one or other nature to guide us. The one is the carnal way, in which we put forth our utmost efforts and resolutions, trusting Christ to help us in doing so. The other the spiritual way, in which, as those who have died, and can do nothing, our one care is to receive Christ day by day, and at every step to let Him live and work in us.

"Despair of purging the flesh or natural man of its sinful lusts and inclinations, and of practising holiness by your willing and resolving to do the best that lieth in your own power, and trusting on the grace of God and Christ to help you in such resolutions and endeavours. Rather resolve to trust on Christ to work in you to will and to do by His own power according to His own good pleasure. They that are convinced of their own sin and misery do commonly first think to tame the flesh, and to subdue and root out its lusts, and to make their corrupt nature to be better-natured and inclined to holiness by their struggling and wrestling with it; and if they can but bring their hearts to a full purpose and resolution to do the best that lieth in them, they hope that by such a resolution they shall be able to achieve great enterprises in the conquests of their lusts and performance of the most difficult duties. It is the great work of some zealous divines in their preachings and writings to stir up people to this resolution, wherein they place the chiefest turningpoint from sin to godliness. And they think that this is not contrary to the life of faith, because they trust in the grace of God through Christ to help them in all such resolutions and endeavours. Thus they endeavour to reform their old state, and to be made perfect in the flesh, instead of putting it off and walking according to the new state in Christ. They trust on low carnal things for holiness, and upon the acts of their own will, their purposes, resolutions, and endeavours, instead of Christ; and they trust to Christ to help them in this carnal way; whereas true faith would teach them that they are nothing, and that they do but labour in vain."

Chapter 30 -- As The Surety Of The Covenant

"Jesus was made a surety of a better testament." -- Heb 7:22

Of the old Covenant, Scripture speaks as not being faultless, and God complains that Israel had not continued in it; and so He regarded them not (Heb.8:7-9). It had not secured its apparent object, in uniting Israel and God: Israel had forsaken Him, and He had not regarded Israel. Therefore God promises to make a New Covenant, free from the faults of the first, and effectual to realize its purpose. If it were to accomplish its end, it would need to secure God's faithfulness to His people, and His people's faithfulness to God. And the terms of the New Covenant expressly declare that these two objects shall be attained. "I will put my laws into their mind": thus God proposes to secure their unchanging faithfulness to Him. "Their sins I will remember no more" (see Heb.8:10-12): thus He assures His unchanging faithfulness to them. A pardoning God and an obedient people: these are the two parties who are to meet and to be eternally united in the New Covenant.

The most beautiful provision of this New Covenant is that of the surety in whom its fulfilment on both parts is guaranteed. Jesus was made the surety of the better covenant. To man He became surety that God would faithfully fulfil His part, so that man could confidently depend upon God to pardon, and accept, and never more forsake. And to God He likewise became surety that man would faithfully fulfil his part, so that God could bestow on him the blessing of the covenant. And the way in which He fulfils His suretyship is this: As one with God, and having the fulness of God dwelling in His human nature, He is personally security to men that God will do what He has engaged. All that God has is secured to us in Him as man. And then, as one with us, and having taken us up as members into His own body, He is security to God that His interests shall be cared for. All that man must be and do is secured in Him. It is the glory of the New Covenant that it has in the Person of the God-man its living surety, its everlasting security. And it can easily be understood how, in proportion as we abide in Him as the surety of the covenant, its objects and its blessings will be realized in us.

We shall understand this best if we consider it in the light of one of the promises of the New Covenant. Take that in Jer.32:40 : "I will make an everlasting covenant with them, that I will not turn away from them, to do them good; but I will put my fear in their hearts, that they shall not depart from me."

With what wonderful condescension the infinite God here bows Himself to our weakness! He is the Faithful and Unchanging One, whose word is truth; and yet more abundantly to show to the heirs of the promise the immutability of His counsel, He binds Himself in the covenant that He will never change: "I will make an everlasting covenant, that I will not turn away from them." Blessed the man who has thoroughly appropriated this, and finds his rest in the everlasting covenant of the Faithful One!

But in a covenant there are two parties. And what if man becomes unfaithful and breaks the covenant? Provision must be made, if the covenant is to be well ordered in all things and sure, that this cannot be, and that man too remain faithful. Man never can undertake to give such an assurance. And see, here God comes to provide for this too. He not only undertakes in the covenant that He will never turn from His people, but also to put His fear in their heart, that they do not depart from Him. In addition to His own obligations as one of the covenanting parties, He undertakes for the other party too: "I WILL CAUSE you to walk in my statutes, and ye shall keep my judgments and do them" (Ezek.36:27). Blessed the man who understands this half of the covenant too! He sees that his security is not in the covenant which he makes with His God, and which he would but continually break again. He finds that a covenant has been made, in which God stands good, not only for Himself, but for man too. He grasps the blessed truth that his part in the covenant is to accept what God has promised to do, and to expect the sure fulfilment of the divine engagement to secure the faithfulness of His people to their God: "I will put my fear in their hearts, that they shall not depart from me."

It is just here that the blessed work comes in of the surety of the covenant, appointed of the Father to see to its maintenance and perfect fulfilment. To Him the Father hath said, "I have given thee for a covenant of the people." And the Holy Spirit testifies, "All the promises of God IN Him are yea, and in Him are Amen, to the glory of God by us." The believer who abides in Him hath a divine assurance for the fulfilment of every promise the covenant ever gave.

Christ was made surety of a better testament. It is as our Melchisedec that Christ is surety (see Heb.7). Aaron and his sons passed away; of Christ it is witnessed that He liveth. He is priest in the power of an endless life. Because He continueth ever, He hath an unchangeable priesthood. And because He ever liveth to make intercession, He can save to the uttermost, He can save completely. It is because Christ is the Ever-living One that His suretyship of the covenant is so effectual. He liveth ever to make intercession, and can therefore save completely. Every moment there rise up from His holy presence to the Father, the unceasing pleadings which secure to His people the powers and the blessings of the heavenly life. And every moment there go out from Him downward to His people, the mighty influences of His unceasing intercession, conveying to them uninterruptedly the power of the heavenly life. As surety with us for the Father's favour, He never ceases to pray and present us before Him; as surety with the Father for us, He never ceases to work, and reveal the Father within us.

The mystery of the Melchisedec priesthood, which the Hebrews were not able to receive (Heb.5:10-14), is the mystery of the resurrection life. It is in this that the glory of Christ as surety of the covenant consists: He ever liveth. He performs His work in heaven in the power of a divine, an omnipotent life. He ever liveth to pray; not a moment that as surety His prayers do not rise Godward to secure the Father's fulfilment to us of the covenant. He performs His work on earth in the power of that same life; not a moment that His answered prayers -- the powers of the heavenly world -- do not flow downward to secure for His Father our fulfilment of the covenant. In the eternal life there are no breaks -- never a moment's interruption; each moment has the power of eternity in it. He ever, every moment, liveth to pray. He ever, every moment, liveth to bless. He can save to the uttermost, completely and perfectly, because He ever liveth to pray.

184

Believer! come and see here how the possibility of abiding in Jesus every moment is secured by the very nature of this ever-living priesthood of your surety. Moment by moment, as His intercession rises up, its efficacy descends. And because Jesus stands good for the fulfilment of the covenant -- "I will put my fear in their heart, and they shall not depart from me" -- He cannot afford to leave you one single moment to yourself. He dare not do so, or He fails of His undertaking. Your unbelief may fail of realizing the blessing; He cannot be unfaithful. If you will but consider Him, and the power of that endless life after which He was made and is a High Priest, your faith will rise to believe that an endless, ever-continuing, unchangeable life of abiding in Jesus, is nothing less than what is waiting you.

It is as we see what Jesus is, and is to us, that the abiding in Him will become the natural and spontaneous result of our knowledge of Him. If His life unceasingly, moment by moment, rises to the Father for us, and descends to us from the Father, then to abide moment by moment is easy and simple. Each moment of conscious intercourse with Him we simply say, "Jesus, surety, keeper, ever-living Saviour, in whose life I dwell, I abide in Thee." Each moment of need, or darkness, or fear, we still say, "O thou great High Priest, in the power of an endless, unchangeable life, I abide in Thee." And for the moments when direct and distinct communion with Him must give place to needful occupations, we can trust His suretyship, His unceasing priesthood, in its divine efficacy, and the power with which He saves to the uttermost, still to keep us abiding in Him.

Chapter 31 -- The Glorified One

"Your life is hid with Christ in God. When Christ, who is our life, shall appear, then shall ye also appear with him in glory." -- Col.3:3-4

He that abides in Christ the Crucified One, learns to know what it is to be crucified with Him, and in Him to be indeed dead unto sin. He that abides in Christ the Risen and Glorified One, becomes in the same way partaker of His resurrection life, and of the glory with which He has now been crowned in heaven. Unspeakable are the blessings which flow to the soul from the union with Jesus in His glorified life.

This life is a life of perfect victory and rest. Before His death, the Son of God had to suffer and to struggle, could be tempted and troubled by sin and its assaults: as the Risen One, He has triumphed over sin; and, as the Glorified One, His humanity has entered into participation of the glory of Deity. The believer who abides in Him as such, is led to see how the power of sin and the flesh are indeed destroyed: the consciousness of complete and everlasting deliverance becomes increasingly clear, and the blessed rest and peace, the fruit of such a conviction that victory and deliverance are an accomplished fact, take possession of the life. Abiding in Jesus, in whom he has been raised and set in the heavenly places, he receives of that glorious life streaming from the Head through every member of the body.

This life is a life in the full fellowship of the Father's love and holiness. Jesus often gave prominence to this thought with His disciples. His death was a going to the Father. He prayed: "Glorify me, O Father, with Thyself, with the glory which I had with Thee." As the believer, abiding in Christ the Glorified One, seeks to realize and experience what His union with Jesus on the throne implies, he apprehends how the unclouded light of the Father's presence is His highest glory and blessedness, and in Him the believer's portion too. He learns the sacred art of always, in fellowship with His exalted Head, dwelling in the secret of the Father's presence. Further, when Jesus was on earth, temptation could still reach Him: in glory, everything is holy, and in perfect harmony with the will of God. And so the believer who abides in Him experiences that in this high fellowship his spirit is sanctified into growing harmony with the Father's will. The heavenly life of Jesus is the power that casts out sin.

This life is a life of loving beneficence and activity. Seated on His throne, He dispenses His gifts, bestows His Spirit, and never ceases in love to watch and to work for those who are His. The believer cannot abide in Jesus the Glorified One, without feeling himself stirred and strengthened to work: the Spirit and the love of Jesus breathe the will and the power to be a blessing to others. Jesus went to heaven with the very object of obtaining power there to bless abundantly. He does this as the heavenly Vine only through the medium of His people as His branches. Whoever, therefore, abides in Him, the Glorified One, bears much fruit, for he receives of the Spirit and the power of the eternal life of his exalted Lord, and becomes the channel through which the fulness of Jesus, who hath been exalted to be a Prince and a Saviour, flows out to bless those around him.

There is one more thought in regard to this life of the Glorified One, and ours in Him. It is a life of wondrous expectation and hope. It is so with Christ. He sits at the right hand of God, expecting till all His enemies be made His footstool, looking forward to the time when He shall receive His full reward, when His glory shall be made manifest, and His beloved people be ever with Him in that glory. The hope of Christ is the hope of His redeemed: "I will come again and take you to myself, that where I am there ye may be also." This promise is as precious to Christ as it ever can be to us. The joy of meeting is surely no less for the coming bridegroom than for the waiting bride. The life of Christ in glory is one of longing expectation: the full glory only comes when His beloved are with Him.

The believer who abides closely in Christ will share with Him in this spirit of expectation. Not so much for the increase of personal happiness, but from the spirit of enthusiastic allegiance to his King, he longs to see Him come in His glory, reigning over every enemy, the fill revelation of God's everlasting love. "Till He come," is the watchword of every true-hearted believer. "Christ shall appear, and we shall appear with Him in glory."

There may be very serious differences in the exposition of the promises of His coming. To one it is plain as day that He is coming very speedily in person to reign on earth, and that speedy coming is his hope and his stay. To another, loving his Bible and his Saviour not less, the coming can mean nothing but the judgment day -- the solemn transition from time to eternity, the close of history on earth, the beginning of heaven; and the thought of that manifestation of his Saviour's glory is no less his joy and his strength. It is Jesus, Jesus coming again, Jesus taking us to Himself, Jesus adored as Lord of all, that is to the whole Church the sum and the centre of its hope.

It is by abiding in Christ the Glorified One that the believer will be quickened to that truly spiritual looking for His coming, which alone brings true blessing to the soul. There is an interest in the study of the things which are to be, in which the discipleship of a school is often more marked than the discipleship of Christ the meek; in which contendings for opinions and condemnation of brethren are more striking than any signs of the coming glory. It is only the humility that is willing to learn from those who may have other gifts and deeper revelations of the truth than we, and the love that always speaks gently and tenderly of those who see not as we do, and the heavenliness that shows that the Coming One is indeed already our life, that will persuade either the Church or the world that this our faith is not in the wisdom of men, but in the power of God. To testify of the Saviour as the Coming One, we must be abiding in and bearing the image of Him as the Glorified One. Not the correctness of the views we hold, nor the earnestness with which we advocate them, will prepare us for meeting Him, but only the abiding in Him. Then only can our being manifested in glory with Him be what it is meant to be -- a transfiguration, a breaking out and shining forth of the indwelling glory that had been waiting for the day of revelation.

Blessed life! "the life hid with Christ in God," "set in the heavenlies in Christ," abiding in Christ the glorified! Once again the question comes: Can a feeble child of dust really dwell in fellowship with the King of glory? And again the blessed answer has to be given: To maintain that union is the very work for which Christ has all power in heaven and earth at His disposal. The blessing will be given to him who will trust his Lord for it, who in faith and confident expectation ceases not to yield himself to be wholly one with Him. It was an act of wondrous though simple faith, in which the soul yielded itself at first to the Saviour. That faith grows up to clearer insight and faster hold of God's truth that we are one with Him in His glory. In that same wondrous faith, wondrously simple, but wondrously mighty, the soul learns to abandon itself entirely to the keeping of Christ's almighty power, and the actings of His eternal life. Because it knows that it has the Spirit of God dwelling within to communicate all that Christ is, it no longer looks upon it as a burden or a work, but allows the divine life to have its way, to do its work; its faith is the increasing abandonment of self, the expectation and acceptance of all that the love and the power of the Glorified One can perform. In that faith unbroken fellowship is maintained, and growing conformity realized. As with Moses, the fellowship makes partakers of the glory, and the life begins to shine with a brightness not of this world.

Blessed life! it is ours, for Jesus is ours. Blessed life! we have the possession within us in its hidden power, and we have the prospect before us in its fullest glory. May our daily lives be the bright and blessed proof that the hidden power dwells within, preparing us for the glory to be revealed. May our abiding in Christ the Glorified One be our power to live to the glory of the Father, our fitness to share to the glory of the Son.

And now,
Little children,
Abide in him,
That, when he shall appear, we may have
Confidence, and not be ashamed
Before him at his coming.

< The End of Abide in Christ>

The True Vine

Meditations for a Month on John 15:1-16.....
(31 Lessons)

By
Rev. Andrew Murray

Moody Press
Chicago

"The mystery which hath been hid from ages, but now is made manifest to His saints: to whom God would make known what is the riches of the glory of this mystery...which is Christ in you, the hope of glory." -- Colossians 1.26,27

ONLY A BRANCH

"I am the vine, ye are the branches." -- John 15.5

"Tis only a little Branch,
A thing so fragile and weak,
But that little Branch hath a message true
To give, could it only speak.

"I'm only a little Branch,
I live by a life not mine,
For the sap that flows through my tendrils small
Is the life-blood of the Vine.

"No power indeed have I
The fruit of myself to bear,
But since I'm part of the living Vine,
Its fruitfulness I share.

"Dost thou ask how I abide?
How this life I can maintain? --
I am bound to the Vine by life's strong band,
And I only need remain.

"Where first my life was given,
In the spot where I am set,

Upborne and upheld as the days go by,
By the stem which bears me yet.

"I fear not the days to come,
I dwell not upon the past,
As moment by moment I draw a life,
Which for evermore shall last.

"I bask in the sun's bright beams,
Which with sweetness fills my fruit,
Yet I own not the clusters hanging there,
For they all come from the root."

A life which is not my own,
But another's life in me:
This, this is the message the Branch would speak,
A message to thee and me.

Oh, struggle not to "abide,"
Nor labor to "bring forth fruit,"
But let Jesus unite thee to Himself,
As the Vine Branch to the root.

So simple, so deep, so strong
That union with Him shall be:
His life shall forever replace thine own,
And His love shall flow through thee.

For His Spirit's fruit is love,
And love shall thy life become,
And for evermore on His heart of love
Thy spirit shall have her home.

      Freda Hanbury

Preface

I have felt drawn to try to write what young Christians might easily apprehend, as a help to them to take up that position in which the Christian life must be a success. It is as if there is not one of the principal temptations and failures of the Christian life that is not met here. The nearness, the all-sufficiency, the faithfulness of the Lord Jesus, the naturalness, the fruitfulness of a life of faith, are so revealed, that it is as if one could with confidence say, Let the parable enter into the heart, and all will be right.

May the blessed Lord give the blessing. May He teach us to study the mystery of the Vine in the spirit of worship, waiting for God's own teaching.

1 The Vine

I am the True Vine -- John 15.1

All earthly things are the shadows of heavenly realities -- the expression, in created, visible forms, of the invisible glory of God. The Life and the Truth are in Heaven; on earth we have figures and shadows of the heavenly truths. When Jesus says: "I am the true Vine," He tells us that all the vines of earth are pictures and emblems of Himself. He is the divine reality, of which they are the created expression. They all point to Him, and preach Him, and reveal Him. If you would know Jesus, study the vine.

How many eyes have gazed on and admired a great vine with its beautiful fruit. Come and gaze on the heavenly Vine till your eye turns from all else to admire Him. How many, in a sunny clime, sit and rest under the shadow of a vine. Come and be still under the shadow of the true Vine, and rest under it from the heat of the day. What countless numbers rejoice in the fruit of the vine! Come, and take, and eat of the heavenly fruit of the true Vine, and let your soul say: "I sat under His shadow with great delight, and His fruit was sweet to my taste."

I am the true Vine. -- This is a heavenly mystery. The earthly vine can teach you much about this Vine of Heaven. Many interesting and beautiful points of comparison suggest themselves, and help us to get conceptions of what Christ meant. But such thoughts do not teach us to know what the heavenly Vine really is, in its cooling shade, and its life-giving fruit. The experience of this is part of the hidden mystery, which none but Jesus Himself, by His Holy Spirit, can unfold and impart.

I am the true Vine. -- The vine is the living Lord, who Himself speaks, and gives, and works all that He has for us. If you would know the meaning and power of that word, do not think to find it by thought or study; these may help to show you what you must get from Him to awaken desire and hope and prayer, but they cannot show you the Vine. Jesus alone can reveal Himself. He gives His Holy Spirit to open the eyes to gaze upon Himself, to open the heart to receive Himself. He must Himself speak the word to you and me.

I am the true Vine. -- And what am I to do, if I want the mystery, in all its heavenly beauty and blessing, opened up to me? With what you already know of the parable, bow down and be still, worship and wait, until the divine Word enters your heart, and you feel His holy presence with you, and in you. The overshadowing of His holy love will give you the perfect calm and rest of knowing that the Vine will do all.

I am the true Vine. -- He who speaks is God, in His infinite power able to enter into us. He is man, one with us. He is the crucified One, who won a perfect righteousness and a divine life for us through His death. He is the glorified One, who from the throne gives His Spirit to make His presence real and true. He speaks -- oh, listen, not to His words only, but to Himself, as He whispers secretly day by day: "I am the true Vine! All that the Vine can ever be to its branch, "I will be to you."

Holy Lord Jesus, the heavenly Vine of God's own planting, I beseech Thee, reveal Thyself to my soul. Let the Holy Spirit, not only in thought, but in experience, give me to know all that Thou, the Son of God, art to me as the true Vine.

2 The Husbandman

And My Father is the Husbandman -- John 15.1

A vine must have a husbandman to plant and watch over it, to receive and rejoice in its fruit. Jesus says: "My Father is the husbandman." He was "the vine of God's planting." All He was and did, He owed to the Father; in all He only sought the Father's will and glory. He had become man to show us what a creature ought to be to its Creator. He took our place, and the spirit of His life before the Father was ever what He seeks to make ours: "Of him, and through him, and to him are all things." He became the true Vine, that we might be true branches. Both in regard to Christ and ourselves the words teach us the two lessons of absolute dependence and perfect confidence.

My Father is the Husbandman. -- Christ ever lived in the spirit of what He once said: "The Son can do nothing of himself." As dependent as a vine is on a husbandman for the place where it is to grow, for its fencing in and watering and pruning. Christ felt Himself entirely dependent on the Father every day for the wisdom and the strength to do the Father's will. As He said in the previous chapter (14:10): "The words that I say unto you, I speak not from Myself; but the Father abiding in Me doeth his works." This absolute dependence had as its blessed counterpart the most blessed confidence that He had nothing to fear: the Father could not disappoint Him. With such a Husbandman as His Father, He could enter death and the grave. He could trust God to raise Him up. All that Christ is and has, He has, not in Himself, but from the Father.

My Father is the Husbandman. -- That is as blessedly true for us as for Christ. Christ is about to teach His disciples about their being branches. Before He ever uses the word, or speaks at all of abiding in Him or bearing fruit, He turns their eyes heavenward to the Father watching over them, and working all in them. At the very root of all Christian life lies the thought that God is to do all, that our work is to give and leave ourselves in His hands, in the confession of utter helplessness and dependence, in the assured confidence that He gives all we need. The great lack of the Christian life is that, even where we trust Christ, we leave God out of the count. Christ came to bring us to God. Christ lived the life of a man exactly as we have to live it. Christ the Vine points to God the Husbandman. As He trusted God, let us trust God, that everything we ought to be and have, as those who belong to the Vine, will be given us from above.

Isaiah said: "A vineyard of red wine; I the Lord do keep it, I will water it every moment; lest any hurt it, I will keep it night and day." Ere we begin to think of fruit or branches, let us have our heart filled with the faith: as glorious as the Vine, is the Husbandman. As high and holy as is our calling, so mighty and loving is the God who will work it all. As surely as the Husbandman made the Vine what it was to be, will He make each branch what it is to be. Our Father is our Husbandman, the Surety for our growth and fruit.

Blessed Father, we are Thy husbandry. Oh, that Thou mayest have honor of the work of Thy hands! O my Father, I desire to open my heart to the joy of this wondrous truth: My Father is the Husbandman. Teach me to know and trust Thee, and to see that the same deep interest with which Thou caredst for and delightedst in the Vine, extends to every branch, to me too.

3 The Branch

Every Branch in me that Beareth Not Fruit, He taketh It away -
- John 15.2

Here we have one of the chief words of the parable -- branch.
A vine needs branches: without branches it can do nothing,
can bear no fruit. As important as it is to know about the Vine,
and the Husbandman, it is to realize what the branch is.
Before we listen to what Christ has to say about it, let us first
of all take in what a branch is, and what it teaches us of our
life in Christ. A branch is simply a bit of wood, brought forth by
the vine for the one purpose of serving it in bearing its fruit. It
is of the very same nature as the vine, and has one life and
one spirit with it. Just think a moment of the lessons this
suggests.

There is the lesson of entire consecration. The branch has but
one object for which it exists, one purpose to which it is
entirely given up. That is, to bear the fruit the vine wishes to
bring forth. And so the believer has but one reason for his
being a branch -- but one reason for his existence on earth --
that the heavenly Vine may through him bring forth His fruit.
Happy the soul that knows this, that has consented to it, and
that says, I have been redeemed and I live for one thing -- as
exclusively as the natural branch exists only to bring forth fruit,
I too; as exclusively as the heavenly Vine exists to bring forth
fruit, I too. As I have been planted by God into Christ, I have
wholly given myself to bear the fruit the Vine desires to bring
forth.

There is the lesson of perfect conformity. The branch is exactly like the vine in every aspect -- the same nature, the same life, the same place, the same work. In all this they are inseparably one. And so the believer needs to know that he is partaker of the divine nature, and has the very nature and spirit of Christ in him, and that his one calling is to yield himself to a perfect conformity to Christ. The branch is a perfect likeness of the vine; the only difference is, the one is great and strong, and the source of strength, the other little and feeble, ever needing and receiving strength. Even so the believer is, and is to be, the perfect likeness of Christ.

There is the lesson of absolute dependence. The vine has its stores of life and sap and strength, not for itself, but for the branches. The branches are and have nothing but what the vine provides and imparts. The believer is called to, and it is his highest blessedness to enter upon, a life of entire and unceasing dependence upon Christ. Day and night, every moment, Christ is to work in him all he needs.

And then the lesson of undoubting confidence. The branch has no cure; the vine provides all; it has but to yield itself and receive. It is the sight of this truth that leads to the blessed rest of faith, the true secret of growth and strength: "I can do all things through Christ which strengtheneth me."

What a life would come to us if we only consented to be branches! Dear child of God, learn the lesson. You have but one thing to do: Only be a branch -- nothing more, nothing less! Just be a branch; Christ will be the Vine that gives all. And the Husbandman, the mighty God, who made the Vine what it is, will as surely make the branch what it ought to be.

Lord Jesus, I pray Thee, reveal to me the heavenly mystery of the branch, in its living union with the Vine, in its claim on all its fullness. And let Thy all-sufficiency, holding and filling Thy branches, lead me to the rest of faith that knows that Thou workest all.

4 The Fruit

Every Branch in me That Beareth Not Fruit, He Taketh It Away
-- John 15.2

Fruit. -- This is the next great word we have: the Vine, the
Husbandman, the branch, the fruit. What has our Lord to say
to us of fruit? Simply this -- that fruit is the one thing the
branch is for, and that if it bear not fruit, the husbandman
takes it away. The vine is the glory of the husbandman; the
branch is the glory of the vine; the fruit is the glory of the
branch; if the branch bring not forth fruit, there is no glory or
worth in it; it is an offense and a hindrance; the husbandman
takes it away. The one reason for the existence of a branch,
the one mark of being a true branch of the heavenly Vine, the
one condition of being allowed by the divine Husbandman to
share the life the Vine is -- bearing fruit.

And what is fruit? Something that the branch bears, not for itself, but for its owner; something that is to be gathered, and taken away. The branch does indeed receive it from the vine sap for its own life, by which it grows thicker and stronger. But this supply for its own maintenance is entirely subordinate to its fulfillment of the purpose of its existence -- bearing fruit. It is because Christians do not understand or accept of this truth, that they so fail in their efforts and prayers to live the branch life. They often desire it very earnestly; they read and meditate and pray, and yet they fail, they wonder why? The reason is very simple: they do not know that fruit-bearing is the one thing they have been saved for. Just as entirely as Christ became the true Vine with the one object, you have been made a branch too, with the one object of bearing fruit for the salvation of men. The Vine and the branch are equally under the unchangeable law of fruit-bearing as the one reason of their being. Christ and the believer, the heavenly Vine and the branch, have equally their place in the world exclusively for one purpose, to carry God's saving love to men. Hence the solemn word: Every branch that beareth not fruit, He taketh it away.

Let us specially beware of one great mistake. Many Christians think their own salvation is the first thing; their temporal life and prosperity, with the care of their family, the second; and what of time and interest is left may be devoted to fruit-bearing, to the saving of men. No wonder that in most cases very little time or interest can be found. No, Christian, the one object with which you have been made a member of Christ's Body is that the Head may have you to carry out His saving work. The one object God had in making you a branch is that Christ may through you bring life to men. Your personal salvation, your business and care for your family, are entirely subordinate to this. Your first aim in life, your first aim every day, should be to know how Christ desires to carry out His purpose in you.

Let us begin to think as God thinks. Let us accept Christ's teaching and respond to it. The one object of my being a branch, the one mark of my being a true branch, the one condition of my abiding and growing strong, is that I bear the fruit of the heavenly Vine for dying men to eat and live. And the one thing of which I can have the most perfect assurance is that, with Christ as my Vine, and the Father as my Husbandman, I can indeed be a fruitful branch.

Our Father, Thou comest seeking fruit. Teach us, we pray Thee, to realize how truly this is the one object of our existence, and of our union to Christ. Make it the one desire of our hearts to be branches, so filled with the Spirit of the Vine, as to bring forth fruit abundantly.

5 More Fruit

And Every Branch That Beareth Fruit, He Cleanseth, That it
May Bear More Fruit -- John 15.2

The thought of fruit is so prominent in the eye of Him who
sees things as they are, fruit is so truly the one thing God has
set His heart upon, that our Lord, after having said that the
branch that bears no fruit is taken away, at once adds: and
where there is fruit, the one desire of the Husbandman is more
fruit. As the gift of His grace, as the token of spiritual vigor, as
the showing forth of the glory of God and of Christ, as the only
way for satisfying the need of the world, God longs and fits for,
more fruit.

More Fruit -- This is a very searching word. As churches and
individuals we are in danger of nothing so much as self-
contentment. The secret spirit of Laodicea -- we are rich and
increased in goods, and have need of nothing -- may prevail
where it is not suspected. The divine warning -- poor and
wretched and miserable -- finds little response just where it is
most needed.

Let us not rest content with the thought that we are taking an equal share with others in the work that is being done, or that men are satisfied with our efforts in Christ's service, or even point to us as examples. Let our only desire be to know whether we are bearing all the fruit Christ is willing to give through us as living branches, in close and living union with Himself, whether we are satisfying the loving heart of the great Husbandman, our Father in Heaven, in His desire for more fruit.

More Fruit -- The word comes with divine authority to search and test our life: the true disciple will heartily surrender himself to its holy light, and will earnestly ask that God Himself may show what there may be lacking in the measure or the character of the fruit he bears. Do let us believe that the Word is meant to lead us on to a fuller experience of the Father's purpose of love, of Christ's fullness, and of the wonderful privilege of bearing much fruit in the salvation of men.

More Fruit -- The word is a most encouraging one. Let us listen to it. It is just to the branch that is bearing fruit that the message comes: more fruit. God does not demand this as Pharaoh the task-master, or as Moses the lawgiver, without providing the means. He comes as a Father, who gives what He asks, and works what He commands. He comes to us as the living branches of the living Vine, and offers to work the more fruit in us, if we but yield ourselves into His hands. Shall we not admit the claim, accept the offer, and look to Him to work it in us?

"That it may bear more fruit": do let us believe that as the owner of a vine does everything to make the fruitage as rich and large as possible, the divine Husbandman will do all that is needed to make us bear more fruit. All He asks is, that we set our heart's desire on it, entrust ourselves to His working and care, and joyfully look to Him to do His perfect work in us. God has set His heart on more fruit; Christ waits to work it in us; let us joyfully look up to our divine Husbandman and our heavenly Vine, to ensure our bearing more fruit.

Our Father which art in Heaven, Thou art the heavenly Husbandman. And Christ is the heavenly Vine. And I am a heavenly branch, partaker of His heavenly life, to bear His heavenly fruit. Father, let the power of His life so fill me, that I may ever bear more fruit, to the glory of Thy name.

6 The Cleansing

Every Branch That Beareth Fruit, He Cleanseth It, That It May
Bear More Fruit -- John 15.2

There are two remarkable things about the vine. There is not a
plant of which the fruit has so much spirit in it, of which spirit
can be so abundantly distilled as the vine. And there is not a
plant which so soon runs into wild wood, that hinders its fruit,
and therefore needs the most merciless pruning. I look out of
my window here on large vineyards: the chief care of the
vinedresser is the pruning. You may have a trellis vine rooting
so deep in good soil that it needs neither digging, nor
manuring, nor watering: pruning it cannot dispense with, if it is
to bear good fruit. Some tree needs occasional pruning; others
bear perfect fruit without any: the vine must have it. And so
our Lord tells us, here at the very outset of the parable, that
the one work the Father does to the branch that bears fruit is:
He cleanseth it, that it may bear more fruit.

Consider a moment what this pruning or cleansing is. It is not the removal of weeds or thorns, or anything from without that may hinder the growth. No; it is the cutting off of the long shoots of the previous year, the removal of something that comes from within, that has been produced by the life of the vine itself. It is the removal of something that is a proof of the vigor of its life; the more vigorous the growth has been, the greater the need for the pruning. It is the honest, healthy wood of the vine that has to be cut away. And why? Because it would consume too much of the sap to fill all the long shoots of last year's growth: the sap must be saved up and used for fruit alone. The branches, sometimes eight and ten feet long, are cut down close to the stem, and nothing is left but just one or two inches of wood, enough to bear the grapes. It is when everything that is not needful for fruit-bearing has been relentlessly cut down, and just as little of the branches as possible has been left, that full, rich fruit may be expected.

What a solemn, precious lesson! It is not to sin only that the cleansing of the Husbandman here refers. It is to our own religious activity, as it is developed in the very act of bearing fruit. It is this that must be cut down and cleansed away. We have, in working for God, to use our natural gifts of wisdom, or eloquence, or influence, or zeal. And yet they are ever in danger of being unduly developed, and then trusted in. And so, after each season of work, God has to bring us to the end of ourselves, to the consciousness of the helplessness and the danger of all that is of man, to feel that we are nothing. All that is to be left of us is just enough to receive the power of the life-giving sap of the Holy Spirit. What is of man must be reduced to its very lowest measure. All that is inconsistent with the most entire devotion to Christ's service must be removed. The more perfect the cleansing and cutting away of all that is of self, the less of surface over which the Holy Spirit is to be spread, so much the more intense can be the concentration of our whole being, to be entirely at the disposal of the Spirit. This is the true circumcision of the heart, the circumcision of Christ. This is the true crucifixion with Christ, bearing about the dying of the Lord Jesus in the body.

Blessed cleansing, God's own cleansing! How we may rejoice in the assurance that we shall bring forth more fruit.

O our holy Husbandman, cleanse and cut away all that there is in us that would make a fair show, or could become a source of self-confidence and glorying. Lord, keep us very low, that no flesh may glory in Thy presence. We do trust Thee to do Thy work.

7 The Pruning Knife

Already Ye Are Clean Because of the Word I Have Spoken Unto You -- John 15.3

What is the pruning knife of this heavenly Husbandman? It is often said to be affliction. By no means in the first place. How would it then fare with many who have long seasons free from adversity; or with some on whom God appears to shower down kindness all their life long? No; it is the Word of God that is the knife, shaper than any two-edged sword, that pierces even to the dividing asunder of the soul and spirit, and is quick to discern the thoughts and intents of the heart. It is only when affliction leads to this discipline of the Word that it becomes a blessing; the lack of this heart-cleansing through the Word is the reason why affliction is so often unsanctified. Not even Paul's thorn in the flesh could become a blessing until Christ's Word -- "My strength is made perfect in weakness" -- had made him see the danger of self-exaltation, and made him willing to rejoice in infirmities.

The Word of God's pruning knife. Jesus says: "Ye are already clean, because of the word I have spoken unto you." How searchingly that word had been spoken by Him, out of whose mouth there went a sharp two-edged sword, as he had taught them! "Except a man deny himself, lose his life, forsake all, hate father and mother, he cannot be My disciple, he is not worthy of Me"; or as He humbled their pride, or reproved their lack of love, or foretold their all forsaking Him. From the opening of His ministry in the Sermon on the Mount to His words of warning in the last night, His Word had tried and cleansed them. He had discovered and condemned all there was of self; they were now emptied and cleansed, ready for the incoming of the Holy Spirit.

It is as the soul gives up its own thoughts, and men's thoughts of what is religion, and yields itself heartily, humbly, patiently, to the teaching of the Word by the Spirit, that the Father will do His blessed work of pruning and cleansing away all of nature and self that mixes with our work and hinders His Spirit. Let those who would know all the Husbandman can do for them, all the Vine can bring forth through them, seek earnestly to yield themselves heartily to the blessed cleansing through the Word. Let them, in their study of the Word, receive it as a hammer that breaks and opens up, as a fire that melts and refines, as a sword that lays bare and slays all that is of the flesh. The word of conviction will prepare for the word of comfort and of hope, and the Father will cleanse them through the Word.

All ye who are branches of the true Vine, each time you read or hear the Word, wait first of all on Him to use it for His cleansing of the branch. Set your heart upon His desire for more fruit. Trust Him as Husbandman to work it. Yield yourselves in simple childlike surrender to the cleansing work of His Word and Spirit, and you may count upon it that His purpose will be fulfilled in you.

Father, I pray Thee, cleanse me through Thy Word. Let it search out and bring to light all that is of self and the flesh in my religion. Let it cut away every root of self-confidence, that the Vine may find me wholly free to receive His life and Spirit. O my holy Husbandman, I trust Thee to care for the branch as much as for the Vine. Thou only art my hope.

8 Abide

Abide in Me, and I in You -- John 15.4

When a new graft is placed in a vine and it abides there, there
is a twofold process that takes place. The first is in the wood.
The graft shoots its little roots and fibers down into the stem,
and the stem grows up into the graft, and what has been
called the structural union is effected. The graft abides and
becomes one with the vine, and even though the vine were to
die, would still be one wood with it. Then there is the second
process, in which the sap of the vine enters the new structure,
and uses it as a passage through which sap can flow up to
show itself in young shoots and leaves and fruit. Here is the
vital union. Into the graft which abides in the stock, the stock
enters with sap to abide in it.

When our Lord says: "Abide in me, and I in you," He points to something analogous to this. "Abide in me": that refers more to that which we have to do. We have to trust and obey, to detach ourselves from all else, to reach out after Him and cling to Him, to sink ourselves into Him. As we do this, through the grace He gives, a character is formed, and a heart prepared for the fuller experience: "I in you," God strengthens us with might by the Spirit in the inner man, and Christ dwells in the heart by faith.

Many believers pray and long very earnestly for the filling of the Spirit and the indwelling of Christ, and wonder that they do not make more progress. The reason is often this, the "I in you" cannot come because the "abide in me" is not maintained. "There is one body and one spirit"; before the Spirit can fill, there must be a body prepared. The graft must have grown into the stem, and be abiding in it before the sap can flow through to bring forth fruit. It is as in lowly obedience we follow Christ, even in external things, denying ourselves, forsaking the world, and even in the body seeking to be conformable to Him, as we thus seek to abide in Him, that we shall be able to receive and enjoy the "I in you." The work enjoined on us: "Abide in me," will prepare us for the work undertaken by Him: "I in you."

In the two parts of the injunction have their unity in that central deep-meaning word "in." There is no deeper word in Scripture. God is in all. God dwells in Christ. Christ lives in God. We are in Christ. Christ is in us: our life taken up into His; His life received into ours; in a divine reality that words cannot express, we are in Him and He in us. And the words, "Abide in me and I in you," just tell us to believe it, this divine mystery, and to count upon our God the Husbandman, and Christ the Vine, to make it divinely true. No thinking or teaching or praying can grasp it; it is a divine mystery of love. As little as we can effect the union can we understand it. Let us just look upon this infinite, divine, omnipotent Vine loving us, holding us, working in us. Let us in the faith of His working abide and rest in Him, ever turning heart and hope to Him alone. And let us count upon Him to fulfill in us the mystery: "Ye in me, and I in you."

Blessed Lord, Thou dost bid me abide in Thee. How can I, Lord, except Thou show Thyself to me, waiting to receive and welcome and keep me? I pray Thee show me how Thou as Vine undertaketh to do all. To be occupied with Thee is to abide in Thee. Here I am, Lord, a branch, cleansed and abiding -- resting in Thee, and awaiting the inflow of Thy life and grace.

9 Except Ye Abide

As the Branch Cannot Bear Fruit of Itself, Except It Abide In the Vine; No More Can Ye, Except Ye Abide in Me -- John 15.4

We know the meaning of the word except. It expresses some indispensable condition, some inevitable law. "The branch cannot bear fruit of itself, except it abide in the vine. No more can ye, except ye abide in me." There is but one way for the branch to bear fruit, there is no other possibility, it must abide in unbroken communion with the vine. Not of itself, but only of the vine, does the fruit come. Christ had already said: "Abide in me"; in nature the branch teaches us the lesson so clearly; it is such a wonderful privilege to be called and allowed to abide in the heavenly Vine; one might have thought it needless to add these words of warning. But no -- Christ knows so well what a renunciation of self is implied in this: "Abide in me"; how strong and universal the tendency would be to seek to bear fruit by our own efforts; how difficult it would be to get us to believe that actual, continuous abiding in Him is an absolute necessity! He insists upon the truth: Not of itself can the branch bear fruit; except it abide, it cannot bear fruit. "No more can ye, except ye abide in me."

But must this be taken literally? Must I, as exclusively, and manifestly, and unceasingly, and absolutely, as the branch abides in the vine, be equally given up to find my whole life in Christ alone? I must indeed. The except ye abide is as universal as the except it abide. The no more can ye admits of no exception or modification. If I am to be a true branch, if I am to bear fruit, if I am to be what Christ as Vine wants me to be, my whole existence must be as exclusively devoted to abiding in Him, as that of the natural branch is to abiding in its vine.

Let me learn the lesson. Abiding is to be an act of the will and the whole heart. Just as there are degrees in seeking and serving God, "not with a perfect heart," or "with the whole heart," so there may be degrees in abiding. In regeneration the divine life enters us, but does not all at once master and fill our whole being. This comes as matter of command and obedience. There is unspeakable danger of our not giving ourselves with our whole heart to abide. There is unspeakable danger of our giving ourselves to work for God, and to bear fruit, with but little of the true abiding, the wholehearted losing of ourselves in Christ and His life. There is unspeakable danger of much work with but little fruit, for lack of this one thing needful. We must allow the words, "not of itself," "except it abide," to do their work of searching and exposing, of pruning and cleansing, all that there is of self-will and self-confidence in our life; this will deliver us from this great evil, and so prepare us for His teaching, giving the full meaning of the word in us: "Abide in me, and I in you."

Our blessed Lord desires to call us away from ourselves and our own strength, to Himself and His strength. Let us accept the warning, and turn with great fear and self-distrust to Him to do His work. "Our life is hid with Christ in God!" That life is a heavenly mystery, hid from the wise even among Christians, and revealed unto babes. The childlike spirit learns that life is given from Heaven every day and every moment to the soul that accepts the teaching: "not of itself," "except it abide," and seeks its all in the Vine. Abiding in the Vine then comes to be nothing more nor less than the restful surrender of the soul to let Christ have all and work all, as completely as in nature the branch knows and seeks nothing but the vine.

Abide in Me. I have heard, my Lord, that with every command, Thou also givest the power to obey. With Thy "rise and walk," the lame man leaped, I accept Thy word, "Abide in me," as a word of power, that gives power, and even now I say, Yea, Lord, I will, I do abide in Thee.

10 The Vine

I am The Vine, Ye Are The Branches -- John 15.5

In the previous verse Christ had just said: "Abide in me." He had then announced the great unalterable law of all branch-life, on earth or in Heaven: "not of itself"; "except it abide." In the opening words of the parable He had already spoken: "I am the vine." He now repeats the words. He would have us understand -- note well the lesson, simple as it appears, it is the key of the abiding life -- that the only way to obey the command, "Abide in me," is to have eye and heart fixed upon Himself. "Abide in me...I am the true vine." Yea, study this holy mystery until you see Christ as the true Vine, bearing, strengthening, supplying, inspiring all His branches, being and doing in each branch all it needs, and the abiding will come of itself. Yes, gaze upon Him as the true Vine, until you feel what a heavenly Mystery it is, and are compelled to ask the Father to reveal it to you by His Holy Spirit. He to whom God reveals the glory of the true Vine, he who sees what Jesus is and waits to do every moment, he cannot but abide. The vision of Christ is an irresistible attraction; it draws and holds us like a magnet. Listen ever to the living Christ still speaking to you, and waiting to show you the meaning and power of His Word: "I am the vine."

How much weary labor there has been in striving to understand what abiding is, how much fruitless effort in trying to attain it! Why was this? Because the attention was turned to the abiding as a work we have to do, instead of the living Christ, in whom we were to be kept abiding, who Himself was to hold and keep us. we thought of abiding as a continual strain and effort -- we forget that it means rest from effort to one who has found the place of his abode. Do notice how Christ said, "Abide in Me; I am the Vine that brings forth, and holds, and strengthens, and makes fruitful the branches. Abide in Me, rest in Me, and let Me do My work. I am the true Vine, all I am, and speak, and do is divine truth, giving the actual reality of what is said. I am the Vine, only consent and yield thy all to Me, I will do all in thee."

And so it sometimes comes that souls who have never been specially occupied with the thought of abiding, are abiding all the time, because they are occupied with Christ. Not that the word abide is not needful; Christ used it so often, because it is the very key to the Christian life. But He would have us understand it in its true sense -- "Come out of every other place, and every other trust and occupation, come out of self with its reasonings and efforts, come and rest in what I shall do. Live out of thyself; abide in Me. Know that thou art in Me; thou needest no more; remain there in Me."

"I am the Vine." Christ did not keep this mystery hidden from His disciples. He revealed it, first in words here, then in power when the Holy Spirit came down. He will reveal it to us too, first in the thoughts and confessions and desires these words awaken, then in power by the Spirit. Do let us wait on Him to show us all the heavenly meaning of the mystery. Let each day, in our quiet time, in the inner chamber with Him and His Word, our chief thought and aim be to get the heart fixed on Him, in the assurance: all that a vine ever can do for its branches, my Lord Jesus will do, is doing, for me. Give Him time, give Him your ear, that He may whisper and explain the divine secret: "I am the vine."

Above all, remember, Christ is the Vine of God's planting, and you are a branch of God's grafting. Ever stand before God, in Christ; ever wait for all grace from God, in Christ; ever yield yourself to bear the more fruit the Husbandman asks, in Christ. And pray much for the revelation of the mystery that all the love and power of God that rested on Christ is working in you too. "I am God's Vine," Jesus says; "all I am I have from Him; all I am is for you; God will work it in you."

I am the Vine. Blessed Lord, speak Thou that word into my soul. Then shall I know that all Thy fullness is for me. And that I can count upon Thee to stream it into me, and that my abiding is so easy and so sure when I forget and lose myself in the adoring faith that the Vine holds the branch and supplies its every need.

11 Ye The Branches

I Am The Vine, Ye Are the Branches -- John 15.5

Christ had already said much of the branch; here He comes to the personal application: "Ye are the branches of whom I have been speaking. As I am the Vine, engaged to be and do all the branches need, so I now ask you, in the new dispensation of the Holy Spirit whom I have been promising you, to accept the place I give you, and to be My branches on earth." The relationship He seeks to establish is an intensely personal one: it all hinges on the two little words I and You. And it is for us as intensely personal as for the first disciples. Let us present ourselves before our Lord, until He speak to each of us in power, and our whole soul feels it: "I am the Vine; you are the branch."

Dear disciple of Jesus, however young or feeble, hear the voice. "You are the branch." You must be nothing less. Let no false humility, no carnal fear of sacrifice, no unbelieving doubts as to what you feel able for, keep you back from saying: "I will be a branch, with all that may mean -- a branch, very feeble, but yet as like the Vine as can be, for I am of the same nature, and receive of the same spirit. A branch, utterly helpless, and yet just as manifestly set apart before God and men, as wholly given up to the work of bearing fruit, as the Vine itself. A branch, nothing in myself, and yet resting and rejoicing in the faith that knows that He will provide for all. Yes, by His grace, I will be nothing less than a branch, and all He means it to be, that through me, He may bring forth His fruit."

You are the branch. -- You need be nothing more. You need not for one single moment of the day take upon you the responsibility of the Vine. You need not leave the place of entire dependence and unbounded confidence. You need, least of all, to be anxious as to how you are to understand the mystery, or fulfill its conditions, or work out its blessed aim. The Vine will give all and work all. The Father, the Husbandman, watches over your union with and growth in the Vine. You need be nothing more than a branch. Only a branch! Let that be your watchword; it will lead in the path of continual surrender to Christ's working, of true obedience to His every command, of joyful expectancy of all His grace.

Is there anyone who now asks: "How can I learn to say this aright, Only be a branch!' and to live it out?" Dear soul, the character of a branch, its strength, and the fruit it bears, depend entirely upon the Vine. And your life as branch depends entirely upon your apprehension of what our Lord Jesus is. Therefore never separate the two words: "I the Vine -- you the branch." Your life and strength and fruit depend upon what your Lord Jesus is! Therefore worship and trust Him; let Him be your one desire and the one occupation of your heart. And when you feel that you do not and cannot know Him aright, then just remember it is part of His responsibility as Vine to make Himself known to you. He does this not in thoughts and conceptions -- no -- but in a hidden growth within the life that is humbly and restfully and entirely given up to wait on Him. The Vine reveals itself within the branch; thence comes the growth and fruit, Christ dwells and works within His branch; only be a branch, waiting on Him to do all; He will be to thee the true Vine. The Father Himself, the divine Husbandman, is able to make thee a branch worthy of the heavenly Vine. Thou shalt not be disappointed.

Ye are the branches. This word, too Lord! O speak it in power unto my soul. Let not the branch of the earthly vine put me to shame, but as it only lives to bear the fruit of the vine, may my life on earth have no wish or aim, but to let Thee bring forth fruit through me.

12 Much Fruit

He That Abideth in Me, and I in Him, the Same Bringeth Forth Much Fruit -- John 15.5

Our Lord had spoken of fruit, more fruit. He now adds the thought: much fruit. There is in the Vine such fullness, the care of the divine Husbandman is so sure of success, that the much fruit is not a demand, but the simple promise of what must come to the branch that lives in the double abiding -- he in Christ, and Christ in him. "The same bringeth forth much fruit." It is certain.

Have you ever noticed the difference in the Christian life between work and fruit? A machine can do work: only life can bear fruit. A law can compel work: only love can spontaneously bring forth fruit. Work implies effort and labor: the essential idea of fruit is that it is the silent natural restful produce of our inner life. The gardener may labor to give his apple tree the digging and manuring, the watering and the pruning it needs; he can do nothing to produce the apple: "The fruit of the Spirit is love, peace, joy." The healthy life bears much fruit. The connection between work and fruit is perhaps best seen in the expression, "fruitful in every good work." (Col. 1.10). It is only when good works come as the fruit of the indwelling Spirit that they are acceptable to God. Under the compulsion of law and conscience, or the influence of inclination and zeal, men may be most diligent in good works, and yet find that they have but little spiritual result. There can be no reason but this -- their works are man's effort, instead of being the fruit of the Spirit, the restful, natural outcome of the Spirit's operation within us.

Let all workers come and listen to our holy Vine as He reveals the law of sure and abundant fruitfulness: "He that abideth in me, and I in him, the same bringeth forth much fruit." The gardener cares for one thing -- the strength and healthy life of his tree: the fruit follows of itself. If you would bear fruit, see that the inner life is perfectly right, that your relation to Christ Jesus is clear and close. Begin each day with Him in the morning, to know in truth that you are abiding in Him and He in you. Christ tells that nothing less will do. It is not your willing and running, it is not by your might or strength, but -- "by my Spirit, saith the Lord." Meet each new engagement, undertake every new work, with an ear and heart open to the Master's voice: "He that abideth in me, beareth much fruit." See you to the abiding; He will see to the fruit, for He will give it in you and through you.

O my brother, it is Christ must do all! The Vine provides the sap, and the life, and the strength: the branch waits, and rests, and receives, and bears the fruit. Oh, the blessedness of being only branches, through whom the Spirit flows and brings God's life to men!

I pray you, take time and ask the Holy Spirit to give you to realize the unspeakably solemn place you occupy in the mind of God. He has planted you into His Son with the calling and the power to bear much fruit. Accept that place. Look much to God, and to Christ, and expect joyfully to be what God has planned to make you, a fruitful branch.

Much fruit! So be it, blessed Lord Jesus. It can be, for Thou art the Vine. It shall be, for I am abiding in Thee. It must be, for Thy Father is the Husbandman that cleanses the branch. Yea, much fruit, out of the abundance of Thy grace.

13 You Can Do Nothing

Apart From Me Ye Can Do Nothing -- John 15.5

In everything the life of the branch is to be the exact counterpart of that of the Vine. Of Himself Jesus had said: "The Son can do nothing of himself." As the outcome of that entire dependence, He could add: "All that the Father doeth, doeth the Son also likewise." As Son He did not receive His life from the Father once for all, but moment by moment. His life was a continual waiting on the Father for all He was to do. And so Christ says of His disciples: "Ye can do nothing apart from me." He means it literally. To everyone who wants to live the true disciple life, to bring forth fruit and glorify God, the message comes: You can do nothing. What had been said: "He that abideth in me, and I in him, the same beareth much fruit," is here enforced by the simplest and strongest of arguments: "Abiding in Me is indispensable, for, you know it, of yourselves you can do nothing to maintain or act out the heavenly life."

231

A deep conviction of the truth of this word lies at the very root of a strong spiritual life. As little as I created myself, as little as I could raise a man from the dead, can I give myself the divine life. As little as I can give it myself, can I maintain or increase it: every motion is the work of God through Christ and His Spirit. It is as a man believes this, that he will take up that position of entire and continual dependence which is the very essence of the life of faith. With the spiritual eye he sees Christ every moment supplying grace for every breathing and every deepening of the spiritual life. His whole heart says Amen to the word: You can do nothing. And just because he does so, he can also say: "I can do all things in Christ who strengtheneth me." The sense of helplessness, and the abiding to which it compels, leads to true fruitfulness and diligence in good works.

Apart from me ye can do nothing. -- What a plea and what a call every moment to abide in Christ! We have only to go back to the vine to see how true it is. Look again at that little branch, utterly helpless and fruitless except as it receives sap from the vine, and learn that the full conviction of not being able to do anything apart from Christ is just what you need to teach you to abide in your heavenly Vine. It is this that is the great meaning of the pruning Christ spoke of -- all that is self must be brought low, that our confidence may be in Christ alone. "Abide in me" -- much fruit! "Apart from me" -- nothing! Ought there to be any doubt as to what we shall choose?

The one lesson of the parable is -- as surely, as naturally as the branch abides in the vine, You can abide in Christ. For this He is the true Vine; for this God is the Husbandman; for this you are a branch. Shall we not cry to God to deliver us forever from the "apart from me," and to make the "abide in me" an unceasing reality? Let your heart go out to what Christ is, and can do, to His divine power and His tender love to each of His branches, and you will say evermore confidently: "Lord! I am abiding; I will bear much fruit. My impotence is my strength. So be it. Apart from Thee, nothing. In Thee, much fruit."

Apart from Me -- you nothing. Lord, I gladly accept the arrangement: I nothing -- Thou all. My nothingness is my highest blessing, because Thou art the Vine, that givest and workest all. So be it, Lord! I, nothing, ever waiting on Thy fullness. Lord, reveal to me the glory of this blessed life.

14 Withered Branches

If a Man Abide Not in Me, He is Cast Forth as a Branch, and is Withered; and They Gather Them, and Cast Them into the Fire, and They are Burned -- John 15.6

The lessons these words teach are very simple and very solemn. A man can come to such a connection with Christ, that he counts himself to be in Him, and yet he can be cast forth. There is such a thing as not abiding in Christ, which leads to withering up and burning. There is such a thing as a withered branch, one in whom the initial union with Christ appears to have taken place, and in whom yet it is seen that his faith was but for a time. What a solemn call to look around and see if there be not withered branches in our churches, to look within and see whether we are indeed abiding and bearing fruit!

And what may be the cause of this "not abiding." With some it is that they never understood how the Christian calling leads to holy obedience and to loving service. They were content with the thought that they had believed, and were safe from Hell; there was neither motive nor power to abide in Christ -- they knew not the need of it. With others it was that the cares of the world, or its prosperity, choked the Word: they had never forsaken all to follow Christ. With still others it was that their religion and their faith was in the wisdom of men, and not in the power of God. They trusted in the means of grace, or in their own sincerity, or in the soundness of their faith in justifying grace; they had never come even to seek an entire abiding in Christ as their only safety. No wonder that, when the hot winds of temptation or persecution blew, they withered away: they were not truly rooted in Christ.

Let us open our eyes and see if there be not withered branches all around us in the churches. Young men, whose confessions were once bright, but who are growing cold. Or old men, who have retained their profession, but out of whom the measure of life there once appeared to be has died out. Let ministers and believers take Christ's words to heart, and see, and ask the Lord whether there is nothing to be done for branches that are beginning to wither. And let the word Abide ring through the Church until every believer has caught it -- no safety but in a true abiding in Christ.

Let each of us turn within. Is our life fresh, and green, and vigorous, bringing forth its fruit in its season? (See Ps. 1.3; 92.13, 14; Jer. 17.7, 8.) Let us accept every warning with a willing mind, and let Christ's "if a man abide not" give new urgency to His "abide in me." To the upright soul the secret of abiding will become ever simpler, just the consciousness of the place in which He has put me; just the childlike resting in my union with Him, and the trustful assurance that He will keep me. Oh, do let us believe there is a life that knows of no withering, that is ever green; and that brings forth fruit abundantly!

Withered! O my Father, watch over me, and keep me, and let nothing ever for a moment hinder the freshness that comes from a full abiding in the Vine. Let the very thought of a withered branch fill me with holy fear and watchfulness.

15 Whatsoever Ye Will

If Ye Abide in Me, and My Words Abide in You, Ask Whatsoever Ye Will, and it Shall be Done Unto You -- John 15.7

The Whole place of the branch in the vine is one of unceasing prayer. Without intermission it is ever calling: "O my vine, send the sap I need to bear Thy fruit." And its prayers are never unanswered: it asks what it needs, what it will, and it is done.

The healthy life of the believer in Christ is equally one of unceasing prayer. Consciously or unconsciously, he lives in continual dependence. The Word of his Lord, "You can do nothing," has taught him that not more unbroken than the continuance of the branch in the vine, must be his asking and receiving. The promise of our text gives us infinite boldness: "Ask whatsoever ye will, and it shall be done unto you."

The promise is given in direct connection with fruit-bearing. Limit it to yourself and your own needs, and you rob it of its power; you rob yourself of the power of appropriating it. Christ was sending these disciples out, and they were ready to give their life for the world; to them He gave the disposal of the treasures of Heaven. Their prayers would bring the Spirit and the power they needed for their work.

The promise is given in direct connection with the coming of the Spirit. The Spirit is not mentioned in the parable, just as little as the sap of the vine is mentioned. But both are meant all through. In the chapter preceding the parable, our Lord had spoken of the Holy Spirit, in connection with their inner life, being in them, and revealing Himself within them (14.15-23). In the next chapter He speaks of the Holy Spirit in connection with their work, coming to them, convincing the world, and glorifying Him (16.7-14). To avail ourselves of the unlimited prayer promises, we must be men who are filled with the Spirit, and wholly given up to the work and glory of Jesus. The Spirit will lead us into the truth of its meaning and the certainty of its fulfillment.

Let us realize that we can only fulfill our calling to bear much fruit, by praying much. In Christ are hid all the treasures men around us need; in Him all God's children are blessed with all spiritual blessings; He is full of grace and truth. But it needs prayer, much prayer, strong believing prayer, to bring these blessings down. And let us equally remember that we cannot appropriate the promise without a life given up for men. Many try to take the promise, and then look round for what they can ask. This is not the way; but the very opposite. Get the heart burdened with the need of souls, and the command to save them, and the power will come to claim the promise.

Let us claim it as one of the revelations of our wonderful life in the Vine: He tells us that if we ask in His name, in virtue of our union with Him, whatsoever it be, it will be done to us. Souls are perishing because there is too little prayer. God's children are feeble because there is too little prayer. We bear so little fruit because there is so little prayer. The faith of this promise would make us strong to pray; let us not rest till it has entered into our very heart, and drawn us in the power of Christ to continue and labor and strive in prayer until the blessing comes in power. To be a branch means not only bearing fruit on earth, but power in prayer to bring down blessing from Heaven. Abiding fully means praying much.

Ask what ye will. O my Lord, why is it that our hearts are so little able to accept these words in their divine simplicity? Oh, give me to see that we need nothing less than this promise to overcome the powers of the world and Satan! Teach us to pray in the faith of this Thy promise.

16 If Ye Abide

If Ye Abide in Me, and My Words, Abide in You, Ask
Whatsoever Ye Will, and it Shall be Done Unto You -- John
15.7

The reason the Vine and its branches are such a true parable
of the Christian life is that all nature has one source and
breathes one spirit. The plant world was created to be to man
an object lesson teaching him his entire dependence upon
God, and his security in that dependence. He that clothes the
lilies will much more cloth us. He that gives the trees and the
vines their beauty and their fruits, making each what He meant
it to be, will much more certainly make us what He would have
us to be. The only difference is what God works in the trees is
by a power of which they are not conscious. He wants to work
in us with our consent. This is the nobility of man, that he has
a will that can cooperate with God in understanding and
approving and accepting what He offers to do.

If ye abide -- Here is the difference between the branch of the
natural and the branch of the spiritual Vine. The former abides
by force of nature: the latter abides, not by force of will, but by
a divine power given to the consent of the will. Such is the
wonderful provision God has made that, what the power of
nature does in the one case, the power of grace will do in the
other. The branch can abide in the Vine.

If ye abide in me...ask whatsoever ye will -- If we are to live a true prayer life, with the love and the power and the experience of prayer marking it, there must be no question about the abiding. And if we abide, there need be no question about the liberty of asking what we will, and the certainty of its being done. There is the one condition: "If ye abide in me." There must be no hesitation about the possibility or the certainty of it. We must gaze on that little branch and its wonderful power of bearing such beautiful fruit until we truly learn to abide.

And what is its secret? Be wholly occupied with Jesus. Sink the roots of your being in faith and love and obedience deep down into Him. Come away out of every other place to abide here. Give up everything for the inconceivable privilege of being a branch on earth of the glorified Son of God in Heaven. Let Christ be first. Let Christ be all. Do not be occupied with the abiding -- be occupied with Christ! He will hold you, He will keep you abiding in Him. He will abide in you.

If ye abide in me, and my words abide in you -- This He gives as the equivalent of the other expression: "I in you. If my words abide in you" -- that is, not only in meditation, in memory, in love, in faith -- all these words enter into your will, your being, and constitute your life -- if they transform your character into their own likeness, and you become and are what they speak and mean -- ask what ye will; it shall be done unto you. Your words to God in prayer will be the fruit of Christ and His words living in you.

Ask what ye will, and it shall be done unto you -- Believe in the truth of this promise. Set yourself to be an intercessor for men; a fruit-bearing intercessor, ever calling down more blessing. Such faith and prayer will help you wonderfully to abide wholly and unceasingly.

If ye abide. Yes, Lord, the power to pray and the power to prevail must depend on this abiding in Thee. As Thou art the Vine, Thou art the divine Intercessor, who breathest Thy spirit in us. Oh, for grace to abide simply and wholly in Thee, and ask great things!

17 The Father Glorified

Herein is My Father Glorified, that Ye Bear Much Fruit -- John 15.8

How can we glorify God? Not by adding to His glory or bringing Him any new glory that He has not. But simply by allowing His glory to shine out through us, by yielding ourselves to Him, that His glory may manifest itself in us and through us to the world. In a vineyard or a vine bearing much fruit, the owner is glorified, as it tells of his skill and care. In the disciple who bears much fruit, the Father is glorified. Before men and angels, proof is given of the glory of God's grace and power; God's glory shines out through him.

This is what Peter means when he writes: "He that ministers, let him minister as of the ability that God giveth, that God in all things may be glorified through Jesus Christ." As a man works and serves in a power which comes from God alone, God gets all the glory. When we confess that the ability came from God alone, he that does the work, and they who see it, equally glorify God. It was God who did it. Men judge by the fruit of a garden of what the gardener is. Men judge of God by the fruit that the branches of the Vine of His planting bears. Little fruit brings little glory to God. It brings no honor to either the Vine or the Husbandman. "That ye bear much fruit, herein is my Father glorified."

We have sometimes mourned our lack of fruit, as a loss to ourselves and our fellow men, with complaints of our feebleness as the cause. Let us rather think of the sin and shame of little fruit as robbing God of the glory He ought to get from us. Let us learn the secret of bringing glory to God, serving of the ability which God giveth. The full acceptance of Christ's Word, "You can do nothing"; the simple faith in God, who worketh all in all; the abiding in Christ through whom the divine Husbandman does His work and gets much fruit -- this is the life that will bring glory to God.

Much fruit -- God asks it; see that you give it. God can be content with nothing less; be you content with nothing less. Let these words of Christ -- fruit, more fruit, much fruit -- abide in you, until you think as He does, and you be prepared to take from Him, the heavenly Vine, what He has for you. Much fruit: herein is my Father glorified. Let the very height of the demand be your encouragement. It is so entirely beyond your power, that it throws you more entirely upon Christ, your true Vine. He can, He will, make it true in you.

Much fruit -- God asks because he needs. He does not ask fruit from the branches of His Vine for show, to prove what He can do. No; He needs it for the salvation of men: it is in that He is to be glorified. Throw yourself in much prayer on your Vine and your Husbandman. Cry to God and your Father to give you fruit to bring to men. Take the burden of the hungry and the perishing on you, as Jesus did when He was moved with compassion, and your power in prayer, and your abiding, and your bearing much fruit to the glory of the Father will have a reality and a certainty you never knew before.

The Father glorified. Blessed prospect -- God glorifying Himself in me, showing forth the glory of His goodness and power in what He works in me, and through me. What a motive to bear much fruit, just as much as He works in me! Father, glorify Thyself in me.

18 True Disciples

Herein is My Father Glorified, that Ye Bear Much Fruit: So Shall Ye Be My Disciples -- John 15.8

And are those who do not bear much fruit not disciples? They may be, but in a backward and immature stage. Of those who bear much fruit, Christ says: "These are My disciples, such as I would have them be -- these are true disciples." Just as we say of someone in whom the idea of manliness is realized: That is a man! So our Lord tells who are disciples after His heart, worthy of the name: Those who bear much fruit. We find this double sense of the word disciple in the Gospel. Sometimes it is applied to all who accepted Christ's teaching. At other times it includes only the inner circle of those who followed Christ wholly, and gave themselves to His training for service. The difference has existed throughout all ages. There have always been a smaller number of God's people who have sought to serve Him with their whole heart, while the majority have been content with a very small measure of the knowledge of His grace and will.

And what is the difference between this smaller inner circle and the many who do not seek admission to it? We find it in the words: much fruit. With many Christians the thought of personal safety, which at their first awakening was a legitimate one, remains to the end the one aim of their religion. The idea of service and fruit is always a secondary and very subordinate one. The honest longing for much fruit does not trouble them. Souls that have heard the call to live wholly for their Lord, to give their life for Him as He gave His for them, can never be satisfied with this. Their cry is to bear as much fruit as they possibly can, as much as their Lord ever can desire or give in them.

Bear much fruit: so shall ye be My disciples -- Let me beg every reader to consider these words most seriously. Be not content with the thought of gradually doing a little more or better work. In this way it may never come. Take the words, much fruit, as the revelation of your heavenly Vine of what you must be, of what you can be. Accept fully the impossibility, the utter folly of attempting it in your strength. Let the words call you to look anew upon the Vine, an undertaking to live out its heavenly fullness in you. Let them waken in you once again the faith and the confession: "I am a branch of the true Vine; I can bear much fruit to His glory, and the glory of the Father."

We need not judge others. But we see in God's Word everywhere two classes of disciples. Let there be no hesitation as to where we take our place. Let us ask Him to reveal to us how He ask and claims a life wholly given up to Him, to be as full of His Spirit as He can make us. Let our desire be nothing less than perfect cleansing, unbroken abiding, closest communion, abundant fruitfulness -- true branches of the true Vine.

The world is perishing, the church is failing, Christ's cause is suffering, Christ is grieving on account of the lack of wholehearted Christians, bearing much fruit. Though you scarce see what it implies or how it is to come, say to Him that you are His branch to bear much fruit; that you are ready to be His disciple in His own meaning of the word.

247

My disciples. Blessed Lord, much fruit is the proof that Thou the true Vine hast in me a true branch, a disciple wholly at Thy disposal. Give me, I pray Thee, the childlike consciousness that my fruit is pleasing to Thee, what Thou countest much fruit.

19 The Wonderful Love

Even as the Father Hath Loved Me, I Also Have Loved you --
John 15.9

Here Christ leaves the language of parable, and speaks
plainly out of the Father. Much as the parable could teach, it
could not teach the lesson of love. All that the vine does for
the branch, it does under the compulsion of a law of nature:
there is no personal living love to the branch. We are in
danger of looking to Christ as a Saviour and a supplier of
every need, appointed by God, accepted and trusted by us,
without any sense of the intensity of personal affection in
which Christ embraces us, and our life alone can find its true
happiness. Christ seeks to point us to this.

And how does He do so? He leads us once again to Himself,
to show us how identical His own life is with ours. Even as the
Father loved Him, He loves us. His life as vine dependent on
the Father was a life in the Father's love; that love was His
strength and His joy; in the power of that divine love resting on
Him He lived and died. If we are to live like Him, as branches
to be truly like our Vine, we must share in this too. Our life
must have its breath and being in a heavenly love as much as
His. What the Father's love was to Him, His love will be to us.
If that love made Him the true Vine, His love can make us true
branches. "Even as the Father hath loved me, so have I loved
you."

Even as the Father hath loved Me -- And how did the Father love Him? The infinite desire and delight of God to communicate to the Son all He had Himself, to take the Son into the most complete equality with Himself, to live in the Son and have the Son live in Him -- this was the love of God to Christ. It is a mystery of glory of which we can form no conception, we can only bow and worship as we try to think of it. And with such a love, with this very same love, Christ longs in an infinite desire and delight to communicate to us all He is and has, to make us partakers of His own nature and blessedness, to live in us and have us live in Himself.

And now, if Christ loves us with such an intense, such an infinite divine love, what is it that hinders it triumphing over every obstacle and getting full possession of us? The answer is simple. Even as the love of the Father to Christ, so His love to us is a divine mystery, too high for us to comprehend or attain to by any effort of our own. It is only the Holy Spirit who can shed abroad and reveal in its all-conquering power without intermission this wonderful love of God in Christ. It is the vine itself that must give the branch its growth and fruit by sending up its sap. It is Christ Himself must by His Holy Spirit dwell in the heart; then shall we know and have in us the love that passeth knowledge.

As the Father loved Me, so have I loved you -- Shall we not draw near to the personal living Christ, and trust Him, and yield all to Him, that He may love this love into us? Just as he knew and rejoiced every hour -- the Father loveth Me -- we too may live in the unceasing consciousness -- as the Father loved Him, so He loves me.

As the Father loved Me, so have I loved you. Dear Lord, I am only beginning to apprehend how exactly the life of the Vine is to be that of the branch too. Thou art the Vine, because the Father loved Thee, and poured His love through Thee. And so Thou lovest me, and my life as branch is to be like Thine, a receiving and a giving out of heavenly love.

250

20 Abide In My Love

Even as the Father Hath Loved Me, I Also Have Loved You:
Abide Ye in My Love -- John 15.9

Abide in My love -- We speak of a man's home as his abode.
Our abode, the home of our soul, is to be the love of Christ.
We are to live our life there, to be at home there all the day:
this is what Christ means our life to be, and really can make it.
Our continuous abiding in the Vine is to be an abiding in His
love.

You have probably heard or read of what is called the higher,
or the deeper life, of the richer or the fuller life, of the life
abundant. And you possibly know that some have told of a
wonderful change, by which their life of continual failure and
stumbling had been changed into a very blessed experience
of being kept and strengthened and made exceeding glad. If
you asked them how it was this great blessing came to them,
many would tell you it was simply this, that they were led to
believe that this abiding in Christ's love was meant to be a
reality, and that they were made willing to give up everything
for it, and then enabled to trust Christ to make it true to them.

The love of the Father to the Son is not a sentiment -- it is a divine life, an infinite energy, an irresistible power. It carried Christ through life and death and the grave. The Father loved Him and dwelt in Him, and did all for Him. So the love of Christ to us too is an infinite living power that will work in us all He delights to give us. The feebleness of our Christian life is that we do not take time to believe that this divine love does really delight in us, and will possess and work all in us. We do not take time to look at the Vine bearing the branch so entirely, working all in it so completely. We strive to do for ourselves what Christ alone can, what Christ, oh, so lovingly, longs to do for us.

And this now is the secret of the change we spoke of, and the beginning of a new life, when the soul sees this infinite love willing to do all, and gives itself up to it. "Abide ye in my love." To believe that, it is possible so to live moment by moment; to believe that everything that makes it difficult or impossible will be overcome by Christ Himself; to believe that Love really means an infinite longing to give itself wholly to us and never leave us; and in this faith to cast ourselves on Christ to work it in us; this is the secret of the true Christian life.

And how to come to this faith? Turn away from the visible if you would see and possess the invisible. Take more time with Jesus, gazing on Him as the heavenly Vine, living in the love of the Father, wanting you to live in His love. Turn away from yourself and your efforts and your faith, if you would have the heart filled with Him and the certainty of His love. Abiding means going out from everything else, to occupy one place and stay there. Come away from all else, and set your heart on Jesus, and His love, that love will waken your faith and strengthen it. Occupy yourself with that love, worship it, wait for it. You may be sure it will reach out to you, and by its power take you up into itself as your abode and your home.

Abide in My love. Lord Jesus, I see it, it was Thy abiding in Thy Father's love that made Thee the true Vine, with Thy divine fullness of love and blessing for us. Oh, that I may even so, as a branch, abide in Thy love, for its fullness to fill me and overflow on all around.

21 Obey And Abide

If Ye Keep My Commandments, Ye Shall Abide In My Love --
John 15.10

In our former meditation reference was made to the entrance
into a life of rest and strength which has often come through a
true insight into the personal love of Christ, and the assurance
that that love indeed meant that He would keep the soul. In
connection with that transition, and the faith that sees and
accepts it, the word surrender or consecration is frequently
used. The soul sees that it cannot claim the keeping of this
wonderful love unless it yields itself to a life of entire
obedience. It sees too that the faith that can trust Christ for
keeping from sinning must prove its sincerity by venturing at
once to trust Him for strength to obey. In that faith it dares to
give up and cut off everything that has hitherto hindered it, and
to promise and expect to live a life that is well pleasing to God.

This is the thought we have here now in our Saviour's teaching. After having in the words, "Abide in my love," spoken of a life in His love as a necessity, because it is at once a possibility and an obligation, He states what its one condition is: "If ye keep my commandments, ye shall abide in my love." This is surely not meant to close the door to the abode of His love which he had just opened up. Not in the most distant way does it suggest the thought which some are too ready to entertain, that as we cannot keep His commandments, we cannot abide in His love. No; the precept is a promise: "Abide in my love," could not be a precept if it were not a promise. And so the instruction as to the way through this open door points to no unattainable ideal; the love that invites to her blessed abode reaches out the hand, and enables us to keep the commandments. Let us not fear, in the strength of our ascended Lord, to take the vow of obedience, and give ourselves to the keeping of His commandments. Through His will, loved and done, lies the path to His love.

Only let us understand well what it means. It refers to our performance of all that we know to be God's will. There may be things doubtful, of which we are not sure. A sin of ignorance has still the nature of sin in it. There may be involuntary sins, which rise up in the flesh, which we cannot control or overcome. With regard to these God will deal in due tome in the way of searching and humbling, and if we be simple and faithful, give us larger deliverance than we dare expect. But all this may be found in a truly obedient soul. Obedience has reference to the positive keeping of the commandments of our Lord, and the performance of His will in everything in which we know it. This is a possible degree of grace, and it is the acceptance in Christ's strength of such obedience as the purpose of our heart, of which our Saviour speaks here. Faith in Christ as our Vine, in His enabling and sanctifying power, fits us for this obedience of faith, and secures a life of abiding in His love.

———

If ye keep My commandments, ye shall abide in My love -- It is the heavenly Vine unfolding the mystery of the life He gives. It is to those abiding in Him to whom He opens up the secret of the full abiding in His love. It is the wholehearted surrender in everything to do His will, that gives access to a life in the abiding enjoyment of His love.

Obey and abide. Gracious Lord, teach me this lesson, that it is only through knowing Thy will one can know Thy heart, and only through doing that will one can abide in Thy love. Lord, teach me that as worthless as is the doing in my own strength, so essential and absolutely indispensable is the doing of faith in Thy strength, if I would abide in Thy love.

22 Ye, Even As I

If Ye Keep My Commandments, Ye Shall Abide in My Love, Even as I have Kept My Father's Commandments, and Abide in His Love -- John 15.10

We have had occasion more than once to speak of the perfect similarity of the vine and the branch in nature, and therefore in aim. Here Christ speaks no longer in a parable, but tells us plainly out of how His own life is the exact model of ours. He had said that it is alone by obedience we can abide in His love. He now tells that this was the way in which He abode in the Father's love. As the Vine, so the branch. His life and strength and joy had been in the love of the Father: it was only by obedience He abode in it. We may find our life and strength and joy in His love all the day, but it is only by an obedience like His we can abide in it. Perfect conformity to the Vine is one of the most precious of the lessons of the branch. It was by obedience Christ as Vine honored the Father as Husbandman; it is by obedience the believer as branch honors Christ as Vine.

Obey and abide -- That was the law of Christ's life as much as it is to be that of ours. He was made like us in all things, that we might be like Him in all things. He opened up a path in which we may walk even as He walked. He took our human nature to teach us how to wear it, and show us how obedience, as it is the first duty of the creature, is the only way to abide in the favor of God and enter into His glory. And now He comes to instruct and encourage us, and asks us to keep His commandments, even as He kept His Father's commandments and abides in His love.

The divine fitness of this connection between obeying and abiding, between God's commandments and His love, is easily seen. God's will is the very center of His divine perfection. As revealed in His commandments, it opens up the way for the creature to grow into the likeness of the Creator. In accepting and doing His will, I rise into fellowship with Him. Therefore it was that the Son, when coming into the world, spoke: "I come to do thy will, O God"! This was the place and this would be the blessedness of the creature. This was what he had lost in the Fall. This was what Christ came to restore. This is what, as the heavenly Vine, He asks of us and imparts to us, that even as He by keeping His Father's commandments abode in His love, we should keep His commandments and abide in His love.

Ye, even as I -- The branch cannot bear fruit except as it has exactly the same life as the Vine. Our life is to be the exact counterpart of Christ's life. It can be, just in such measure as we believe in Him as the Vine, imparting Himself and His life to His branches. "Ye, even as I," the Vine says: one law, one nature, one fruit. Do let us take from our Lord the lesson of obedience as the secret of abiding. Let us confess that simple, implicit, universal obedience has taken too little the place it should have. Christ died for us as enemies, when we were disobedient. He took us up into His love; now that we are in Him, His Word is: "Obey and abide; ye, even as I." Let us give ourselves to a willing and loving obedience. He will keep us abiding in His love.

258

Ye, even as I. O my blessed Vine, who makest the branch in everything partake of Thy life and likeness, in this too I am to be like Thee: as Thy life in the Father's love through obedience, so mine in Thy love! Saviour, help me, that obedience may indeed be the link between Thee and me.

23 Joy

These Things Have I Spoken Unto You, That My Joy May Be in You, and That Your Joy May Be Fulfilled -- John 15.11

If any one asks the question, "How can I be a happy Christian?" our Lord's answer is very simple: "These things," about the Vine and the branches, "I have spoken to you, that my joy may be in you, and that your joy may be fulfilled." "You cannot have My joy without My life. Abide in Me, and let Me abide in you, and My joy will be in you." All healthy life is a thing of joy and beauty; live undividedly the branch life; you will have His joy in full measure.

To many Christians the thought of a life wholly abiding in Christ is one of strain and painful effort. They cannot see that the strain and effort only come, as long as we do not yield ourselves unreservedly to the life of Christ in us. The very first words of the parable are not yet opened up to them: "I am the true Vine; I undertake all and provide for all; I ask nothing of the branch but that it yields wholly to Me, and allows Me to do all. I engage to make and keep the branch all that it ought to be." Ought it not to be an infinite and unceasing joy to have the Vine thus work all, and to know that it is none less than the blessed Son of God in His love who is each moment bearing us and maintaining our life?

That My joy may be in you -- We are to have Christ's own joy in us. And what is Christ's own joy? There is no joy like love. There is no joy but love. Christ had just spoken of the Father's love and His own abiding in it, and of His having loved us with that same love. His joy is nothing but the joy of love, of being loved and of loving. It was the joy of receiving His Father's love and abiding in it, and then the joy of passing on that love and pouring it out on sinners. It is this joy He wants us to share: the joy of being loved of the Father and of Him; the joy of in our turn loving and living for those around us. This is just the joy of being truly branches: abiding in His love, and then giving up ourselves in love to bear fruit for others. Let us accept His life, as He gives it in us as the Vine, His joy will be ours: the joy of abiding in His love, the joy of loving like Him, of loving with His love.

And that your joy may be fulfilled -- That it may be complete, that you may be filled with it. How sad that we should so need to be reminded that as God alone is the fountain of all joy, "God our exceeding joy," the only way to be perfectly happy is to have as much of God, as much of His will and fellowship, as possible! Religion is meant to be in everyday life a thing of unspeakable joy. And why do so many complain that it is not so? Because they do not believe that there is no joy like the joy of abiding in Christ and in His love, and being branches through whom He can pour out His love on a dying world.

Oh, that Christ's voice might reach the heart of every young Christian, and persuade him to believe that His joy is the only true joy, that His joy can become ours and truly fill us, and that the sure and simple way of living in it is -- only this -- to abide as branches in Him our heavenly Vine. Let the truth enter deep into us -- as long as our joy is not full, it is a sign that we do not yet know our heavenly Vine aright; every desire for a fuller joy must only urge us to abide more simply and more fully in His love.

My joy -- your joy. In this too it is: as the Vine, so the branch; all the Vine in the branch. Thy joy is our joy -- Thy joy in us, and our joy fulfilled. Blessed Lord, fill me with Thy joy -- the joy of being loved and blessed with a divine love; the joy of loving and blessing others.

24 Love One Another

This is My Commandment, That Ye Love One Another -- John 15.12

God is love. His whole nature and perfection is love, living not for Himself, but to dispense life and blessing. In His love He begat the Son, that He might give all to Him. In His love He brought forth creatures that He might make them partakers of His blessedness.

Christ is the Son of God's love, the bearer, the revealer, the communicator of that love. His life and death were all love. Love is His life, and the life He gives. He only lives to love, to live out His life of love in us, to give Himself in all who will receive Him. The very first thought of the true Vine is love -- living only to impart His life to the branches.

The Holy Spirit is the Spirit of love. He cannot impart Christ's life without imparting His love. Salvation is nothing but love conquering and entering into us; we have just as much of salvation as we have of love. Full salvation is perfect love.

No wonder that Christ said: "A new commandment I give unto you"; "This is my commandment" -- the one all-inclusive commandment -- "that ye love one another." The branch is not only one with the vine, but with all its other branches; they drink one spirit, they form one body, they bear one fruit. Nothing can be more unnatural than that Christians should not love one another, even as Christ loved them. The life they received from their heavenly Vine is nothing but love. This is the one thing He asks above all others. "Hereby shall all men know that ye are my disciples...love one another." As the special sort of vine is known by the fruit it bears, the nature of the heavenly Vine is to be judged of by the love His disciples have to one another.

See that you obey this commandment. Let your "obey and abide" be seen in this. Love your brethren as the way to abide in the love of your Lord. Let your vow of obedience begin here. Love one another. Let your intercourse with the Christians in your own family be holy, tender, Christlike love. Let your thoughts of the Christians round you be, before everything, in the spirit of Christ's love. Let your life and conduct be the sacrifice of love -- give your self up to think of their sins or their needs, to intercede for them, to help and to serve them. Be in your church or circle the embodiment of Christ's love. The life Christ lives in you is love; let the life in which you live it out be all love.

But, man, you write as if all this was so natural and simple and easy. Is it at all possible thus to live and thus to love? My answer is: Christ commands it: you must obey. Christ means it: you must obey, or you cannot abide in His love.

But I have tried and failed. I see no prospect of living like Christ. Ah! that is because you have failed to take in the first word of the parable -- "I am the true Vine: I give all you need as a branch, I give all I myself have." I pray you, let the sense of past failure and present feebleness drive you to the Vine. He is all love. He loves to give. He gives love. He will teach you to love, even as He loved.

Love one another. Dear Lord Jesus, Thou art all love; the life Thou gavest us is love; Thy new commandment, and Thy badge of discipleship is, "Love one another." I accept the charge: with the love with which Thou lovest me, and I love Thee, I will love my brethren.

25 Even As I Have Loved You

This is My Commandment, That Ye Love One Another, Even as I Have Loved You -- John 15.12

This is the second time our Lord uses the expression -- Even as I. The first time it was of His relation to the Father, keeping His commandments, and abiding in His love. Even so we are to keep Christ's commandments, and abide in His love. The second time He speaks of His relation to us as the rule of our love to our brethren: "Love one another, as I have loved you." In each case His disposition and conduct is to be the law for ours. It is again the truth we have more than once insisted on -- perfect likeness between the Vine and the branch.

Even as I -- But is it not a vain thing to imagine that we can keep His commandments, and love the brethren, even as He kept His Father's, and as He loved us? And must not the attempt end in failure and discouragement? Undoubtedly, if we seek to carry out the injunction in our strength, or without a full apprehension of the truth of the Vine and its branches. But if we understand that the "even as I" is just the one great lesson of the parable, the one continual language of the Vine to the branch, we shall see that it is not the question of what we feel able to accomplish, but of what Christ is able to work in us. These high and holy commands -- "Obey, even as I! Love, even as I" -- are just meant to bring us to the consciousness of our impotence, and through that to waken us to the need and the beauty and the sufficiency of what is provided for us in the Vine. We shall begin to hear the Vine speaking every moment to the branch: "Even as I. Even as I: My life is your life; and have a share in all My fullness; the Spirit in you, and the fruit that comes from you, is all just the same as in Me. Be not afraid, but let your faith grasp each "Even as I" as the divine assurance that because I live in you, you may and can live like Me."

But why, if this really be the meaning of the parable, if this really be the life a branch may live, who do so few realize it? Because they do not know the heavenly mystery of the Vine. They know much of the parable and its beautiful lessons. But the hidden spiritual mystery of the Vine in His divine omnipotence and nearness, bearing and supplying them all the day -- this they do not know, because they have not waited on God's Spirit to reveal it to them.

Love one another, even as I have loved you -- "Ye, even as I."
How are we to begin if we are really to learn the mystery?
With the confession that we need to be brought to an entirely
new mode of life, because we have never yet known Christ as
the Vine in the completeness of His quickening and
transforming power. With the surrender to be cleansed from all
that is of self, and detached from all that is in the world, to live
only and wholly as Christ lived for the glory of the Father. And
then with the faith that this "even as I" is in very deed what
Christ is ready to make true, the very life the Vine will maintain
in the branch wholly dependent upon Him.

Even as I. Ever again it is, my blessed Lord, as the Vine, so
the branch -- one life, one spirit, one obedience, one joy, one
love.

Lord Jesus, in the faith that Thou art my Vine, and that I am
Thy branch, I accept Thy command as a promise, and take
Thy "even as I" as the simple revelation of what Thou dost
work in me. Yea, Lord, as Thou hast loved, I will love.

26 Christ's Friendship: Its Origin

Greater Love Hath No Man Than This, That a Man Lay Down His Life for His Friends -- John 15.13

In the three following verses our Lord speaks of His relation to His disciples under a new aspect -- that of friendship. He point us to the love in which it on His side has its origin (v.13): to the obedience on our part by which it is maintained (v.14); and then to the holy intimacy to which it leads (v.15).

Our relation to Christ is one of love. In speaking of this previously, He showed us what His love was in its heavenly glory; the same love with which the Father had loved Him. Here we have it in its earthly manifestation -- lay down His life for us. "Greater love hath no man than this, that a man lay down his life for his friends." Christ does indeed long to have us know that the secret root and strength of all He is and does for us as the Vine is love. As we learn to believe this, we shall feel that here is something which we not only need to think and know about, but a living power, a divine life which we need to receive within us. Christ and His love are inseparable; they are identical. God is love, and Christ is love. God and Christ and the divine love can only be known by having them, by their life and power working within us. "This is eternal life, that they know thee"; there is no knowing God but by having the life; the life working in us alone gives the knowledge. And even so the love; if we would know it, we must drink of its living stream, we must have it shed forth by the Holy Spirit in us.

"Greater love hath no man than this, that a man give his life for his friends." The life is the most precious thing a man has; the life is all he is; the life is himself. This is the highest measure of love: when a man gives his life, he hold nothing back, he gives all he has and is. It is this our Lord Jesus wants to make clear to us concerning His mystery of the Vine; with all He has He has placed Himself at our disposal. He wants us to count Him our very own; He wants to be wholly our possession, that we may be wholly His possession. He gave His life for us in death not merely as a passing act, that when accomplished was done with; no, but as a making Himself ours for eternity. Life for life; He gave His life for us to possess that we might give our life for Him to possess. This is what is taught by the parable of the Vine and the branch, in their wonderful identification, in their perfect union.

It is as we know something of this, not by reason or imagination, but deep down in the heart and life, that we shall begin to see what ought to be our life as branches of the heavenly Vine. He gave Himself to death; He lost Himself, that we might find life in Him. This is the true Vine, who only lives to live in us. This is the beginning and the root of that holy friendship to which Christ invites us.

Great is the mystery of godliness! Let us confess our ignorance and unbelief. Let us cease from our own understanding and our own efforts to master it. Let us wait for the Holy Spirit who dwells within us to reveal it. Let us trust His infinite love, which gave its life for us, to take possession and rejoice in making us wholly its own.

His life for His friends. How wonderful the lessons of the Vine, giving its very life to its branches! And Jesus gave His life for His friends. And that love gives itself to them and in them. My heavenly Vine, oh, teach me how wholly Thou longest to live in me!

27 Christ's Friendship: Its Evidence

Ye Are My Friends, if Ye Do the Things Which I Command You -- John 15.14

Our Lord has said what He gave as proof of His friendship: He gave His life for us. He now tells us what our part is to be -- to do the things which He commands. He gave His life to secure a place for His love in our hearts to rule us; the response His love calls us to, and empowers us for, is that we do what He commands us. As we know the dying love, we shall joyfully obey its commands. As we obey the commands, we shall know the love more fully. Christ had already said: "If ye keep my commandments, ye shall abide in my love." He counts it needful to repeat the truth again: the one proof of our faith in His love, the one way to abide in it, the one mark of being true branches is -- to do the things which He commands us. He began with absolute surrender of His life for us. He can ask nothing less from us. This alone is a life in His friendship.

This truth, of the imperative necessity of obedience, doing all that Christ commands us, has not the place in our Christian teaching and living that Christ meant it to have. We have given a far higher place to privilege than to duty. We have not considered implicit obedience as a condition of true discipleship. The secret thought that it is impossible to do the things He commands us, and that therefore it cannot be expected of us, and a subtle and unconscious feeling that sinning is a necessity have frequently robbed both precepts and promises of their power. The whole relation to Christ has become clouded and lowered, the waiting on His teaching, the power to hear and obey His voice, and through obedience to enjoy His love and friendship, have been enfeebled by the terrible mistake. Do let us try to return to the true position, take Christ's words as most literally true, and make nothing less the law of our life: "Ye are my friends, if ye do the things that I command you." Surely our Lord asks nothing less than that we heartily and truthfully say: "Yea, Lord, what Thou dost command, that will I do."

These commands are to be done as a proof of friendship. The power to do them rests entirely in the personal relationship to Jesus. For a friend I could do what I would not for another. The friendship of Jesus is so heavenly and wonderful, it comes to us so as the power of a divine love entering in and taking possession, the unbroken fellowship with Himself is so essential to it, that it implies and imparts a joy and a love which make the obedience a delight. The liberty to claim the friendship of Jesus, the power to enjoy it, the grace to prove it in all its blessedness -- all come as we do the things He commands us.

Is not the one thing needful for us that we ask our Lord to reveal Himself to us in the dying love in which He proved Himself our friend, and then listen as He says to us: "Ye are My friends." As we see what our Friend has done for us, and what as unspeakable blessedness it is to have Him call us friends, the doing His commands will become the natural fruit of our life in his love. We shall not fear to say: "Yea, Lord, we are Thy friends, and do what Thou dost command us."

———

273

If ye do. Yes, it is in doing that we are blessed, that we abide in His love, that we enjoy His friendship. "If ye do what I command you!" O my Lord, let Thy holy friendship lead me into the love of all Thy commands, and let the doing of Thy commands lead me ever deeper into Thy friendship.

28 Christ's Friendship: Its Intimacy

No Longer Do I Call You Servants; for the Servant Knoweth Not What His Lord Doeth: But I Have Called You Friends; for All Things That I Heard From My Father, I Have Made Known Unto You -- John 15.15

The highest proof of true friendship, and one great source of its blessedness, is the intimacy that holds nothing back, and admits the friend to share our inmost secrets. It is a blessed thing to be Christ's servant; His redeemed ones delight to call themselves His slaves. Christ had often spoken of the disciples as His servants. In His great love our Lord now says: "No longer do I call you servants"; with the coming of the Holy Spirit a new era was to be inaugurated. "The servant knoweth not what his Lord doeth" -- he has to obey without being consulted or admitted into the secret of all his master's plans. "But, I have called you friends, for all things I heard from my Father I have made known unto you." Christ's friends share with Him in all the secrets the Father has entrusted to Him.

Let us think what this means. When Christ spoke of keeping His Father's commandments, He did not mean merely what was written in Holy Scripture, but those special commandments which were communicated to Him day by day, and from hour to hour. It was of these He said: "The Father loveth the Son, and showeth him all things that he doeth, and he will show him greater things." All that Christ did was God's working. God showed it to Christ, so that He carried out the Father's will and purpose, not, as man often does, blindly and unintelligently, but with full understanding and approval. As one who stood in God's counsel, He knew God's plan.

And this now is the blessedness of being Christ's friends, that we do not, as servants, do His will without much spiritual insight into its meaning and aim, but are admitted, as an inner circle, into some knowledge of God's more secret thoughts. From the Day of Pentecost on, by the Holy Spirit, Christ was to lead His disciples into the spiritual apprehension of the mysteries of the kingdom, of which He had hitherto spoken only by parables.

Friendship delights in fellowship. Friends hold council. Friends dare trust to each other what they would not for anything have others know. What is it that gives a Christian access to this holy intimacy with Jesus? That gives him the spiritual capacity for receiving the communications Christ has to make of what the Father has shown Him? "Ye are my friends if ye do what I command you." It is loving obedience that purifies the soul. That refers not only to the commandments of the Word, but to that blessed application of the Word to our daily life, which none but our Lord Himself can give. But as these are waited for in dependence and humility, and faithfully obeyed, the soul becomes fitted for ever closer fellowship, and the daily life may become a continual experience: "I have called you friends; for all things I have heard from my Father, I have made known unto you."

I have called you friends. What an unspeakable honor! What a heavenly privilege! O Saviour, speak the word with power into my soul: "I have called you My friend, whom I love, whom I trust, to whom I make known all that passes between my Father and Me."

29 Election

Ye Did Not Choose Me, But I Chose You, and Appointed You That Ye Should Go and Bear Fruit -- John 15.16

The branch does not choose the vine, or decide on which vine it will grow. The vine brings forth the branch, as and where it will. Even so Christ says: "Ye did not choose me, but I chose you." But some will say is not just this the difference between the branch in the natural and in the spiritual world, that man has a will and a power of choosing, and that it is in virtue of his having decided to accept Christ, his having chosen Him as Lord, that he is now a branch? This is undoubtedly true. And yet it is only half a truth. The lesson of the Vine, and the teaching of our Lord, points to the other half, the deeper, the divine side of our being in Christ. If He had not chosen us, we had never chosen Him. Our choosing Him was the result of His choosing us, and taking hold of us. In the very nature of things, it is His prerogative as Vine to choose and create His own branch. We owe all we are to "the election of grace." If we want to know Christ as the true Vine, the sole origin and strength of the branch life, and ourselves as branches in our absolute, most blessed, and most secure dependence upon Him, let us drink deep of this blessed truth: "Ye did not choose me, but I chose you."

And with what view does Christ say this? That they may know what the object is for which He chose them, and find, in their faith in His election, the certainty of fulfilling their destiny. Throughout Scripture this is the great object of the teaching of election. "Predestinated to be conformed to the image of his son." (to be branches in the image and likeness of the Vine). "Chosen that we should be holy." "Chosen to salvation, through sanctification of the Spirit." "Elect in sanctification of the Spirit unto obedience." Some have abused the doctrine of election, and others, for fear of its abuse, have rejected it, because they have overlooked this teaching. They have occupied themselves with its hidden origin in eternity, with the inscrutable mysteries of the counsels of God instead of accepting the revelation of its purpose in time, and the blessings it brings into our Christian life.

Just think what these blessings are. In our verse Christ reveals His twofold purpose in choosing us to be His branches: that we may bear fruit on earth, and have power in prayer in Heaven. What confidence the thought that He has chosen us for this gives, that He will not fail to fit us for carrying out His purpose! What assurance that we can bear fruit that will abide, and can pray so as to obtain! What a continual call to the deepest humility and praise, to the most entire dependence and expectancy! He would not choose us for what we are not fit for, or what He could not fit us for. He has chosen us; this is the pledge, He will do all in us.

Let us listen in silence of soul to our holy Vine speaking to each of us: "You did not choose Me!" And let us say, "Yea, Lord, but I chose You! Amen, Lord!" Ask Him to show what this means. In Him, the true Vine, your life as branch has its divine origin, its eternal security, and the power to fulfill His purpose. From Him to whose will of love you owe all, you may expect all. In Him, His purpose, and His power, and His faithfulness, in His love let me abide.

278

I chose you. Lord, teach me what this means -- that Thou hast set Thy heart on me, and chosen me to bear fruit that will abide, and to pray prayer that will prevail. In this Thine eternal purpose my soul would rest itself and say: "What He chose me for I will be, I can be, I shall be."

30 Abiding Fruit

I Chose You, and Appointed You, That Ye Should Go and Bear Fruit, and That Your Fruit Should Abide -- John 15.16

There are some fruits that will not keep. One sort of pears or apples must be used at once; another sort can be kept over till next year. So there is in Christian work some fruit that does not last. There may be much that pleases and edified, and yet there is no permanent impression made on the power of the world or the state of the Church. On the other hand, there is work that leaves its mark for generations or for eternity. In it the power of God makes itself lastingly felt. It is the fruit of which Paul speaks when he describes the two styles of ministry: "My preaching was not in persuasive words of wisdom, but in demonstrations of the Spirit and of power; that your faith should not stand in the wisdom of men, but in the power of God." The more of man with his wisdom and power, the less of stability; the more of God's Spirit, the more of a faith standing in God's power.

Fruit reveals the nature of the tree from which it comes. What is the secret of bearing fruit that abides? The answer is simple. It is as our life abides in Christ, as we abide in Him, that the fruit we bear will abide. The more we allow all that is of human will and effort to be cut down short and cleansed away by the divine Husbandman, the more intensely our being withdraws itself from the outward that God may work in us by His Spirit; that is, the more wholly we abide in Christ, the more will our fruit abide.

What a blessed thought! He chose you, and appointed you to bear fruit, and that your fruit should abide. He never meant one of His branches to bring forth fruit that should not abide. The deeper I enter into the purpose of this His electing grace, the surer my confidence will become that I can bring forth fruit to eternal life, for myself and others. The deeper I enter into this purpose of His electing love, the more I will realize what the link is between the purpose from eternity, and the fruit to eternity: the abiding in Him. The purpose is His, He will carry it out; the fruit is His, He will bring it forth; the abiding is His, He will maintain it.

Let everyone who professes to be a Christian worker, pause. Ask whether you are leaving your mark for eternity on those around you. It is not your preaching or teaching, your strength of will or power to influence, that will secure this. All depends on having your life full of God and His power. And that again depends upon your living the truly branchlike life of abiding -- very close and unbroken fellowship with Christ. It is the branch, that abides in Him, that brings forth much fruit, fruit that will abide.

Blessed Lord, reveal to my soul, I pray Thee, that Thou hast chosen me to bear much fruit. Let this be my confidence, that Thy purpose can be realized -- Thou didst choose me. Let this be my power to forsake everything and give myself to Thee. Thou wilt Thyself perfect what Thou hast begun. Draw me so to dwell in the love and the certainty of that eternal purpose, that the power of eternity may posses me, and the fruit I bear may abide.

That ye may bear fruit. O my heavenly Vine, it is beginning to dawn upon my soul that fruit, more fruit -- much fruit -- abiding fruit is the one thing Thou hast to give me, and the one thing as branch I have to give Thee! Here I am. Blessed Lord, work out Thy purpose in me; let me bear much fruit, abiding fruit, to thy glory.

---

31 Prevailing Prayer

I Appointed You That Ye Should Go and Bear Fruit, and That Your Fruit Should Abide: That Whatsoever Ye Shall Ask of the Father in My Name, He May Give It You -- John 15.16

In the first verse of our parable, Christ revealed Himself as the true Vine, and the Father as the Husbandman, and asked for Himself and the Father a place in the heart. Here, in the closing verse, He sums up all His teaching concerning Himself and the Father in the twofold purpose for which He had chosen them. With reference to Himself, the Vine, the purpose was, that they should bear fruit. With reference to the Father, it was, that whatsoever they should ask in His name, should be done of the Father in Heaven. As fruit is the great proof of the true relation to Christ, so prayer is of our relation to the Father. A fruitful abiding in the Son, and prevailing prayer to the Father, are the two great factors in the true Christian life.

That whatsoever ye shall ask of the Father in my name, he may give it you. -- These are the closing words of the parable of the Vine. The whole mystery of the Vine and its branches leads up to the other mystery -- that whatsoever we ask in His name the Father gives! See here the reason of the lack of prayer, and of the lack of power in prayer. It is because we so little live the true branch life, because we so little lose ourselves in the Vine, abiding in Him entirely, that we feel so little constrained to much prayer, so little confident that we shall be heard, and so do not know how to use His name as the key to God's storehouse. The Vine planted on earth has reached up into Heaven; it is only the soul wholly and intensely abiding in it, can reach into Heaven with power to prevail much. Our faith in the teaching and the truth of the parable, in the truth and the life of the Vine, must prove itself by power in prayer. The life of abiding and obedience, of love and joy, of cleansing and fruit-bearing, will surely lead to the power of prevailing prayer.

Whatsoever ye shall ask -- The promise was given to disciples who were ready to give themselves, in the likeness of the true Vine, for their fellow men. This promise was all their provision for their work; they took it literally, they believed it, they used it, and they found it true. Let us give ourselves, as branches of the true Vine, and in His likeness, to the work of saving men, of bringing forth fruit to the glory of God, and we shall find a new urgency and power to pray and to claim the "whatsoever ye ask." We shall waken to our wonderful responsibility of having in such a promise the keys to the King's storehouses given us, and we shall not rest till we have received bread and blessing for the perishing.

"I chose you, that ye may bring forth fruit, and that your fruit may abide; that whatsoever ye shall ask of the Father in my name, he may give it to you." Beloved disciple, seek above everything to be a man of prayer. Here is the highest exercise of your privilege as a branch of the Vine; here is the full proof of your being renewed in the image of God and His Son; here is your power to show how you, like Christ, live not for yourself, but for others; here you enter Heaven to receive gifts for men; here your abiding in Christ has led to His abiding in you, to use you as the channel and instrument of His grace. The power to bear fruit for men has been crowned by power to prevail with God.

"I am the vine, my Father is the Husbandman." Christ's work in you is to bring you so to the Father that His Word may be fulfilled in you: "At that day ye shall ask in my name; and I say not that I will pray the Father for you; for the Father himself loveth you." The power of direct access to the Father for men, the liberty of intercession claiming and receiving blessing for them in faith, is the highest exercise of our union with Christ. Let all who would truly and fully be branches give themselves to the work of intercession. It is the one great work of Christ the Vine in Heaven, the source of power for all His work. Make it your one great work as branch: it will be the power of all your work.

In My name. Yes, Lord, in Thy name, the new name Thou hast given Thyself here, the true Vine. As a branch, abiding in Thee in entire devotion, in full dependence, in perfect conformity, in abiding fruitfulness, I come to the Father, in Thee, and He will give what I ask. Oh, let my life be one of unceasing and prevailing intercession! Amen!

< The End of The True Vine >

Get Discounts From My Bookshelf

You can tab on this page to sign in to get discounts from My Bookshelf.

Tab Here: Get Discounts from my Bookshelf

Made in the USA
San Bernardino, CA
21 September 2017